Field Guide to

DREAMS

How to Identify and Interpret the Symbols in Your Dreams

By Kelly Regan

QUIRK BOOKS

PHILADELPHIA

DISCLAIMER

The dream world is wide and varied. While we have taken care to represent a large variety of types of dreams, the author and publisher cannot guarantee this guide addresses every possible kind worldwide.

Library of Congress Cataloging in Publication Number: 2006901933

ISBN-10: 1-59474-019-4
ISBN-13: 978-1-59474-019-0

Printed in Singapore

Typeset in Adobe Garamond, Franklin Gothic, and Impact

Designed by Karen Onorato
Illustrations by Derek Bacon
Iconography by Karen Onorato
Edited by Erin Slonaker
Production management by Stephanie O'Neill McKenna

Distributed in North America by Chronicle Books
85 Second Street
San Francisco, CA 94105

10 9 8 7 6 5 4 3 2 1

Quirk Books
215 Church Street
Philadelphia, PA 19106
www.quirkbooks.com

Contents

1   *Introduction*
2   *Why Do We Dream?*
3   *A Brief History of Dream Analysis*
6   *Do-It-Yourself Analysis:*
    Tips for Keeping a Dream Journal

FIELD GUIDE TO DREAMS

8   Accident with Airplane, Train, Car, or Boat
11 Airplane
13 Aliens
16 Angels
17 Animal, Attack by Wild
21 Animals
24 Attic
26 Basement
28 Beach/Ocean
31 Bed, Something Under
34 Biblical Figures and Religious Icons
36 Boat
39 Brain
41 Car Trouble/Driving Problems
43 Cave
46 Celebrities
48 Chased, Being
51 Child, Forgetting or Misplacing
53 City
55 Communication Breakdown

57	Computers
61	Connections, Missed
64	Corridors/Hallways
66	Crime, Committing
70	Crime, Victim of
73	Death of Loved One (Unrelated to Actual Death)
76	Death, Your Own
79	Deceased Loved One, Visit from
81	Desert Island
84	Drowning/Breathing Underwater
87	Ears
90	Elevators, Stairs, and Ladders
94	Elimination, Inappropriate or Inconvenient
98	End of the World
101	Exam/Public Performance
103	Eyes
107	Falling
109	Father
112	Feet, Legs, and Shoes
116	Fingers and Hands
120	Fire/Being Burned
124	Flying
126	Glass, Broken
129	Hair
132	Heart
134	Historical Figures
136	Home, Childhood
138	Hospital
140	The Impossible Task

142	Infidelity
145	Insects
148	Jungle
151	Kitchen
153	Liver
155	Lost, Being
158	Mechanical Malfunction
160	Monsters
163	Mother
166	Mouth and Teeth
169	Mud
172	Natural Disasters: Earthquakes, Hurricanes, Tornadoes, and Volcanoes
175	Nudity, Public
178	Paralysis/Running in Slow Motion
181	Partner/Spouse
183	Police Officers
187	Pregnancy/Giving Birth
190	Prison
193	Purse or Wallet, Lost
194	Rain
197	Rivers
199	Rooms, Secret
202	Rooms, Unused
204	Sex, Gender Reversal
206	Sex, Interrupted/Nowhere to Make Love
208	Sex in Public
211	Sex with Someone You Know (Not Your Partner)
215	Sex with Stranger
218	Swamp

219 Teeth Falling Out
222 Treasure, Buried
225 Tunnel
226 Vehicle That Isn't a Vehicle
228 War Zone
230 Water
233 Weapons: Bombs, Clubs, Guns, and Knives
236 Wounds

239 *Glossary*
256 *Sources*
260 *Index*
281 *Acknowledgments*

Introduction

"A dream is a theater in which the dreamer himself is the scene, the player, the prompter, the producer, the author, the public, and the critic."—Carl Jung

We all sleep. We all dream. From the dawn of civilization, humans have struggled to understand the meanings behind their dreams. Are they messages from the gods? Premonitions of the future? Repercussions from a too-spicy dinner? After decades of sleep research, scientists are still, for the most part, unsure what function dreaming serves in the brain. What they do know is that dreaming is, at once, a biological necessity and a psychological enigma.

Field Guide to Dreams explores more than eighty of the most popular dreams and dream images. You'll read about a dream's most common manifestations and the period in your life when the dream is most likely to occur. This book gives you clues to a dream's meaning and tells you what it means if you have the same dream time and again. You'll hear what Freud and Jung might say about a particular vision and discover a dream's sometimes strange, often illuminating historical and cultural context.

If you've always wondered about that dream where you are unprepared for an exam, the one where a giant bear chases you through the forest, or the one where all of your teeth fall out, wonder no more (see pp. 101, 17, and 219, respectively). Even if your particular dream isn't deconstructed in these pages, *Field Guide to Dreams* gives you the clues to look for and the questions you need to ask in order to arrive at the hidden meaning behind even the most bizarre nighttime imaginations.

Why Do We Dream?

The short answer is, nobody knows. Here's what science tells us so far. Studies have shown that adults dream, off and on, for a total of about an hour and a half every night. Researchers in the 1950s discovered, in monitoring brain wave activity, that most dreams take place during Stage 1 sleep, also called rapid eye movement (REM) sleep. In this stage, the eyes dart back and forth under the lids; respiration, pulse, and blood pressure fluctuate wildly; and brain wave activity most resembles that in waking life. Paradoxically, during this stage the body almost always remains completely still. REM sleep is actually the "lightest" and least restful of the four stages of sleep. As morning nears, the time spent in REM sleep grows longer—one reason why we are more likely to remember the dreams we have just before waking. Interestingly, humans are not the only animals to dream; most every mammal (and, some believe, birds) engage in REM sleep as well.

So what is the biological purpose of dreaming? Sleep scientists differ widely on this point. Some believe dreams are simply images generated from the random firing of nerve impulses—the neurological equivalent of a music video. But babies in utero spend virtually every moment in REM sleep, and young children can experience as much as eight hours of REM sleep a night, lending credence to the theory that dreaming serves some sort of critical developmental or repair function in the brain. Other researchers have analyzed magnetic resonance imaging (MRI) scans and discovered that the areas of the brain most active during dream sleep are the emotional centers. This finding points to a need to move beyond purely scientific data to ask the metaphysical question, what role does dreaming play in our psychological lives?

A Brief History of Dream Analysis

The earliest known written record of dream interpretation is the Chester Beatty papyrus, an ancient Egyptian dream manual dating from 2000 BCE. Egyptians believed the god Bes regulated dreams, and they routinely offered sacrifices to keep nightmares at bay. Early civilizations thought dreams were messages sent directly from the gods and that they were intended to warn of future danger, answer questions, or chastise immoral or impious behavior. Both ancient Egyptians and Greeks visited dream temples to "incubate" their dreams; they made sacrifices and slept in the temple until the gods graced them with a vision that offered the guidance they sought. Similarly, in native civilizations of North America and Australia, a young man's rite of passage into adulthood involved traveling alone into the wilderness, fasting, and sometimes ingesting hallucinogenic plants to induce a dream state; the resulting vision would then be interpreted by tribal elders. Many Eastern philosophies believed that a person's soul left this plane altogether during sleep and traveled across the dream realm—a world just as "real" as the waking-life world. In this sense, the only difference between sleep and death was that the soul would reenter its sleeping body before waking.

The Greek philosopher Plato foreshadowed Sigmund Freud by almost two thousand years in claiming that dreams expressed instinctual wishes shaped by a primal force inside of us. Aristotle believed that dreams referenced only the physical body as extensions of our sensory perception—that eating certain foods or suffering certain illnesses would prompt very specific dreams. Perhaps the most famous of the ancient dream philosophers is Artemidorus, the author of *Oneirocritica*, one of the earliest recorded works of dream interpretation. Artemidorus believed that all dreams fell into two categories: those that were entirely frivolous and without significance, and those that predicted the future. Unlike his contemporaries, who believed that dreams were straightforward messages from the gods, Artemidorus expressed great appreciation for the way dreams communicated via highly personal metaphors—an insight that predates similar groundbreaking work by Sigmund Freud, the father of modern psychoanalysis, almost eighteen hundred years later.

Medieval Christians feared their dreams, believing them to be the devil's invitation to sin—a curious assumption, given the frequency of divine dream visions recounted in both the Old and New Testaments of the Bible. By the dawn of the European Enlightenment, philosophers had rejected the divine-messenger theory of dreaming, making the reason-based argument that dreams were a byproduct of both waking-life thoughts and physiological symptoms, the latter a nod to Aristotle's mind-body dream equation. But it was the nineteenth-century Romantic movement—with its insistence on the unconscious mind as the source of all creativity, art, and even dreams—that clearly foreshadowed Freud's work.

Dream analysis took a quantum leap forward with the publication of Freud's landmark 1900 work, *The Interpretation of Dreams*. In it, Freud consolidated several concepts popular with his psychologist contemporaries and argued that all dreams were motivated by the desire to fulfill an unconscious wish, usually a wish that was aggressive or sexual in nature and repressed or disguised from the conscious mind for reasons of self-preservation. Freud famously called dreams "the royal road to the unconscious." For him, the key to unlocking a dream's meaning was to dig for the content of the underlying, secret wish, which he did using techniques of free association. Freud's revolutionary insight that our minds harbor thoughts and urges that are not consciously accessible—but that these same urges are often expressed emotionally through dreams—transformed the intellectual landscape.

Freud's psychoanalytic theory assumed a mind at perpetual war with itself—evading scrutiny, masking one's true feelings. Carl Jung, on the other hand, pursued a more revelatory psychoanalytic process. One of Freud's early disciples, Jung ultimately rejected Freud's assumption that repressed sexual urges were the motivating force behind all human behavior. Jung believed the human psyche sought balance and reconciliation, achieved by understanding and accepting the different aspects of the self—good, bad, and ugly. Acknowledging the darker impulses of our unconscious was a necessary step on the road to individuation, or self-knowledge.

Jung also positioned the individual psyche within the larger context of ancestral history in developing the notion of the collective unconscious—a reflexive connection to humanity's universal wellspring of knowledge and experience. Jung believed this knowledge was expressed in the dream world through characters and situations called archetypes. (Key terms from Freud's and Jung's dream theories are explained in the Glossary, pp. 239–255.)

Most contemporary dream analysis builds on the work of psychologists such as Fritz Perls, founder of Gestalt therapy, and Alfred Adler, a proponent of cognitive therapy. Both rejected the notion of imposing meanings on a dream from without—either through a paternalistic, Freudian interrogation or through a more Jungian insistence on the universality of experience. Modern-day dream theorists recommend a more collaborative analytic endeavor, in which the subject is invited to associate dream images and plotlines with events in his daily life as a way to personalize the meanings of a dream.

Do-It-Yourself Analysis:
Tips for Keeping a Dream Journal

Everyone dreams. When people say, "I rarely dream," what they mean is, "I rarely remember my dreams upon waking." Remembering your dreams, like most other things in life, is a learned skill. Here are a few tips to get you started.

- **Initiate a dialogue with your unconscious mind.** Even something as simple as saying to yourself, out loud, before you go to sleep, "I will remember my dreams tonight," may help you recall a scene or two.

- **Keep a pad and pen on your bedside table.** If you wake from a dream in the middle of the night, it's easy to jot down a few salient phrases before nodding back off—you'd be surprised at the things you remember in the moment that would have evaporated had you waited until morning for a recap.

- **Learn to speak your particular dream language.** The unconscious mind loves to communicate in metaphors, symbols, and puns, all of which have highly personal, and often hilarious, meanings for the individual dreamer. A fair bit of decoding will be necessary, but have patience; you'll be amazed at the nimble ways in which your mind selects anecdotes, emotions, and snatches of dialogue from everyday life and fashions them into a compelling, dense dream narrative.

- **Don't judge yourself.** Dreams often tackle disturbing subjects such as death, sex, and violence. Unless you are on trial for a capital crime, dreaming you have committed a murder (p. 66) doesn't make you a criminal in real life. Your unconscious is using metaphor to get a message across; generally speaking, the more powerful and disturbing the dream images, the more intense the emotions they represent.

- **Know the right questions to ask.** Even if you only took sketchy notes during the night, before you get out of bed in the morning, try to flesh out the details of your dream. Treat it as a short story that needs summarizing. In your recap, focus on the setting, the main characters, and the plot, as well as any prominent smells, sights, sounds, colors, or emotional impressions. With recurring dreams, it's fascinating to note the slight variations from dream to dream.

- **Personalize your analysis.** The dream interpretations in this book are by no means one-size-fits-all. Your life experience, your emotional baggage, your family history—all of these things inform the content of and message behind your dreams. When decoding a dream, the most important question you can ask yourself is, "Does this scenario correspond to a situation I'm experiencing right now in my waking life? And if so, how?"

- As you become more comfortable navigating your inner landscape, **try lucid dreaming**, a learned technique in which the dreamer retains some level of consciousness during sleep in order to control the content and progression of a dream. Some experts believe that lucid dreams can reap great emotional benefits. For example, in a dream of being chased by some sinister creature (p. 48), lucid dreamers might stop running, turn around, and ask the creature, "Why are you chasing me?" The answer could surprise you, and would likely be a big step in defusing the anxiety that prompted the dream in the first place.

Field Guide to Dreams

1. **ACCIDENT WITH AIRPLANE, TRAIN, CAR, OR BOAT**

Common Manifestations: You are traveling via plane, train, car, or ship, when it becomes clear that you are in danger of an accident. Perhaps a plane malfunctions in flight, a train jumps a track or runs away, a car spins out of control, or a boat begins to sink. The primary sensation is of watching the accident happen in slow motion, feeling terrified and powerless to stop what appears to be a fatal wreck.

Variations: Perhaps you're unconsciously mirroring a scene from a classic disaster movie: The vehicle is out of control and the pilot/driver/conductor is incapacitated or unable to navigate any longer. You have to step in and take control in order to survive. (In earlier times, you might have dreamt of a runaway stagecoach.)

Occurrence: As with many nightmares, this dream arises during times of significant personal or professional stress.

The Spin: In dreams, modes of transportation often have enormous personal significance; different vehicles may symbolize a love relationship, your body, your personal autonomy, even your life as a whole. So car (or train, or airplane, or boat) trouble can signify not only turbulence in waking life, but an inability to deal with the crisis. The specific type of vehicle—and the type of crash—hints at additional psychological dimensions. Are you struggling to keep your finances afloat? Has your boss been shooting down your ideas? Are you trying to save a relationship that is ready to crash and burn? Is an addiction to drugs or alcohol careening out of control, like a car with no brakes? Or is your life stuck in a rut that you can't break out of, like a train speeding down the track?

It also might be helpful to examine your reaction to the dream crash. Was your life-or-death fate in someone else's hands, or did you jump in to save yourself and avert the accident? Did you bail out before impact, or go down with the ship? Analyzing your role in the accident may help you better understand your reactions to stress and help you find a way to get your life back on track, as it were.

If Recurrent:	It's time to take control of your life!
What Freud Would Say:	Similar to dreams of missing a train (p. 61), which Freud believed were anxiety dreams about the fear of death, dreams of vehicular crashes could easily be interpreted as an expression of Thanatos, or the death wish. Freud also believed that ships and "vessels of all kinds" were dream symbols for the uterus.

What Jung Would Say:	In his book *Dreams*, Jung argued that the type of vehicle that appears in a transportation-related dream "illustrates the . . . manner in which the dreamer . . . lives his psychic life." Jung finds significance in whether the method of transportation is individual or collective, self-propelled or mechanical. People traveling in airplanes are "flown by an unknown pilot" and "borne along on intuitions emanating from the unconscious." But a person who takes a dream ride on a tram or other public transportation "moves or behaves just like everybody else."
Cultural Context:	Nightmares about transportation accidents speak to a primal fear of losing control; unfortunately, this nightmare is also the one most likely to come true in waking life. The frequent refrain holds true: Traveling by car is far more dangerous than traveling by airplane. According to the National Transportation Safety Board, auto accidents cause about forty thousand deaths each year in the United States, compared with only about two hundred deaths per year from airline crashes. In the United States, 1 out of every 6,800 drivers dies in an auto accident. The rate for U.S. airline passengers is 1 in 1.6 million. The survival rate may be lower for an airplane crash, but the fact remains that airplanes don't crash as often as cars do.
Related Images:	Airplane (p. 11); Boat (p. 36); Car Trouble/ Driving Problems (p. 41); Connections, Missed

(p. 61); Flying (p. 124); Vehicle That Isn't a Vehicle (p. 226)

2.   **AIRPLANE**

Common
Manifestations:
You are flying in an airplane, either a commercial jet-liner or a small, buzzy aircraft. The world whizzes by outside your window as you are transported somewhere new and far away.

Variations:
The nightmare version of this scenario is to dream your plane is about to crash (p. 8). Also common are anxiety dreams about arriving late to the airport and missing your flight (p. 61).

Occurrence:
It's possible that a plane-crash dream could arise post-traumatically for certain crash survivors. But more likely, as with many nightmares, this dream arises during times of significant personal or professional stress.

The Spin:

In dreams, modes of transportation often have enormous personal significance; different vehicles may symbolize a love relationship, your body, your personal autonomy, or even your life as a whole. Airplanes—quick, powerful, able to bring new worlds within reach—are associated with the freedom and transience of birds. According to dream analyst Gillian Holloway, airplanes, which travel through the air, can also symbolize the realm of ideas and speech. Therefore, relentless dreams of airplane crashes could indicate you're worried that someone might shoot down your ideas or that you'll "crash and burn" with an important project.

If Recurrent: Perhaps it's time to enroll in a frequent flyer program.

What Freud   Similar to dreams of missing a train (p. 61), which
Would Say: Freud believed were anxiety dreams about the fear of death, dreams of airplane crashes could easily be interpreted as an expression of Thanatos, or the death wish.

What Jung   In his book *Dreams*, Jung argued that the type of
Would Say: vehicle that appears in a transportation-related dream "illustrates the . . . manner in which the dreamer . . . lives his psychic life." Jung found significance in whether the method of transportation was individual or collective, self-propelled or mechanical. People in airplanes, for example, are "flown by an unknown pilot" and "borne along on intuitions emanating from the unconscious."

Cultural   Humans have dreamt of flying (see p. 124) for thou-
Context: sands of years. But in waking life, even minds as ingenious as Leonardo da Vinci (whose notebooks contained an early prototype for the helicopter) had been unable to construct a heavier-than-air machine

that could generate enough lift and propulsion to overcome gravity's inexorable pull. In the early twentieth century, however, brothers Wilbur and Orville Wright used insights gained from their experience as bicycle repairmen to decipher the mechanics of airplane construction and engineering—indeed, the chain used in their first airplane engine was taken from a bicycle. The innovation of the Wright brothers was to emphasize navigational control of the machine, not simply to generate enough lift and propulsion for takeoff. They proved to be savvy marketers and businessmen as well, conducting experiments in deep secrecy until they could secure both a patent for the technology and lucrative military contracts. Though originally from Dayton, Ohio, they chose Kitty Hawk, North Carolina, as the site for their experiments not just for the area's strong, steady winds, but because it afforded them the seclusion they needed to perfect their craft design.

Related Images: Accident with Airplane, Train, Car, or Boat (p. 8); Connections, Missed (p. 61); Flying (p. 124); Vehicle That Isn't a Vehicle (p. 226)

3.   **ALIENS**

Common
Manifestations: It's *War of the Worlds* all over again, only this time, Tom Cruise is nowhere to be found. Aliens have landed on

Earth, and you're face to face with a few of them. This could be a dream of trying to communicate with these space creatures, or you could simply be kidnapped and returned to the "mother ship," where you await all sorts of, you know, *probing*. It seems unbelievable, and it will be, because you realize no one was there to vouch for the sighting.

The Spin:

Most psychoanalysts believe that any sort of dream monster represents particular aspects of your personality that might feel dangerous or compulsive. Depicting those aspects as aliens underscores just how scary and unrecognizable you believe those impulses to be. Try to deconstruct the storyline to determine what role these aliens play in your dream. Can you communicate with them? What do they want from you? Are they humanoid, or more primitive? Starting a dialogue with these outlandish creatures is the first step in discovering who, or what emotions, they are intended to portray.

If Recurrent:

Perhaps a trip to Roswell, New Mexico, is in order?

What Freud
Would Say:

Freud did not address dreams of alien beings per se. But he did observe that monsters or other beasts that appear in dreams usually represent repressed urges that scare or intimidate the dreamer. Freud speculated, not surprisingly, that wild creatures symbolized sexual aggression and power. He also believed that the dreamer turned this repressed urge into an entirely different creature to disassociate from it and alleviate the anxiety that such feelings cause.

What Jung Would Say:

Jung did not specifically address dreams of alien creatures, although he believed every person's psyche was connected to a collective unconscious that extends beyond the individual realm into what is intuited by shared experience. For Jung, dreams about aliens would no doubt be a likely indication that something powerful in your unconscious is pushing its way to the surface, demanding to be reckoned with. One of the foundations of Jung's world of mystical symbolism and the collective unconscious is the notion of the hero's journey; in this case, the hero must identify and conquer his inner demons (or inner aliens) to progress toward self-knowledge, or individuation.

Cultural Context:

This type of dream perfectly illustrates the reflexive level of discomfort and fear humans have when faced with something perceived as "other." The most simplistic popular science fiction (think Will Smith in *Independence Day*) cultivates a black-and-white worldview premised on the absolute hostility of a society not our own. On the earthly plane, racism, sexism, and crimes of intolerance are, at their very essence, a repudiation of empathy and a violent repression of difference.

Related Images: Animal, Attack by Wild (p. 17); Animals (p. 21); Chased, Being (p. 48); Monsters (p. 160); Paralysis/ Running in Slow Motion (p. 178)

4.   **ANGELS**

Common Manifestations: An angel calls upon you to deliver a message. The angel could manifest as a loved one who is deceased (p. 79), or it could be a more generically divine presence. But the character of the messenger makes you sit up and take serious note of the message, whatever it may be. You wake feeling blessed and profoundly moved.

Variations: Your vision could also encompass other religious figures or icons (p. 34).

The Spin: Dreams of angels can have a transformative impact, whether you perceive the visitation to be an authentic spiritual vision or simply a powerful, positive metaphor. As a dream symbol, angels trigger reactions of trust and hope and serve as a conduit for the kind of revelations that can effect immediate psychological change in the dreamer.

If Recurrent: Take heed of the message, because forces upstairs (or inside) are sending in the big guns to deliver it.

What Freud Would Say:	Freud, an atheist, believed all religion to be an illusion, a form of cultural neurosis resulting from childhood or primitive guilt over the Oedipus complex.

What Jung Would Say:	Jung had strong personal faith and believed religion helped put a person in touch with the archetypes and traditions of the collective unconscious—as long as one's faith did not block the opportunity for psychological growth. Contemporary Jungian analysts believe that angels appearing in dreams highlight the more spiritual aspects of your psyche, aspects you are only now beginning to recognize and understand.

Cultural Context:	The English word *angel* is derived from the Greek *ángelos*, meaning "messenger." In both Christian and Islamic religious traditions, angels are viewed as the messengers and ministers of God.

Related Images:	Biblical Figures and Religious Icons (p. 34); Death of Loved One (Unrelated to Actual Death) (p. 73); Deceased Loved One, Visit from (p. 79); Historical Figures (p. 134)

 5.

ANIMAL, ATTACK BY WILD

Common Manifestations:	Although the reason may be unclear, you are threatened, chased, or attacked by a wild animal. The culprit may be an alligator, bear, lion, tiger, shark, wild dog—any

creature, really. The common thread in this dream is the ferociousness and single-mindedness with which the animal approaches you. The encounter spikes your adrenaline; you wake up awash in anxiety and fear.

Occurrence:

This dream, like the one of monsters hiding in the closet (p. 160), is extremely common in childhood, although it can recur in adulthood as well. Some studies have indicated that wild animal dreams are more common in male children than female children.

The Spin:

Wild animals are clear metaphors for the unconscious urges inside all of us. Often, as you contemplate the plot of the dream, you realize that the focus of your fear seems not to be the physical danger, but that you're in such close proximity to something unpredictable that can't be controlled. In this way, the dream is often about the fear of harboring, and keeping in check, anything that would be considered uncultivated social or sexual behavior. For children, wild-animal dreams serve as a type of placeholder symbol for any new worries or stresses that need processing.

Although the habitual appearance of specific animals (p. 21) in your dreams might hint at deeper symbolism, the type of animal that attacks you is perhaps less significant than the behavior it exhibits in the dream. Dream expert Gayle Delaney recommends taking a moment to consider the personality and behavior of the animal. Did it appear with deadly stealth out of nowhere, or stomp and growl, announcing itself from miles away? Was it possible to communicate with this animal, or was it not responsive? Asking these questions might help you equate the dream behavior with a similar experience you're having with a person or situation in waking life.

What Freud Would Say: The dream of being pursued and threatened by wild animals usually pointed to a dreamer afraid of repressed passionate impulses. In fact, the wild beast itself represented a person consumed by those uncontrollable urges. Freud speculated that the wild animal could symbolize the libido and its untapped power; or that a dreamer might compartmentalize his neurosis or desire and, in the dream, turn it into a different creature to disassociate and alleviate anxiety.

What Jung Would Say: Jung wrote at great length about wild animals, each with its own mythic and cultural symbolism. As a phenomenon, however, he considered them dream archetypes of the Shadow self—symbols of the mysteries of the unconscious mind, or what he called the "dark center." According to Jungian dream analyst Jeremy Taylor, the more ominous or life-threatening the dream encounter, the more likely that the dreamer is disconnected from his intuitions and instincts in waking life. But Taylor also asserts that remembering the dream is a positive indication that the dreamer intends to tackle these issues, at least on some level.

Cultural
Context:

Although the dream of being attacked by something large, wild, and fierce is terrifying, it rarely reflects a serious waking-life threat. In Western societies, the specter of wild animal attacks is, for the most part, extremely remote. Large concentrations of the population live on highly developed swaths of land; people rarely encounter dangerous wild animals outside of zoo or circus settings. Those most likely to tussle with big, dangerous critters such as bears, wolves, mountain lions, and moose live in rural, wooded areas or mountain regions with little human infrastructure. In Asian countries such as India, Nepal, China, and Bangladesh, the most common animal attacks come from tigers and leopards. Many of these animals have either escaped from preserves or, because shrinking habitats mean fewer natural prey, are near starvation and forced to enter populated areas in search of livestock or, occasionally, small children to feed on.

In general, so-called wild animals are almost always more afraid of you than you are of them. In the United States, national park rangers recommend making noise while hiking along park trails—whistling, singing, or jangling a soda can filled with pebbles—in order to announce your presence. Why? Many attacks take place only after an animal is surprised, feels threatened, or is inadvertently separated from its young. If you make enough noise, the animals should steer clear of confrontation.

The most common form of fatal wild encounter in coastal areas is a shark attack—more specifically, attacks by bull sharks, the species most likely to troll shallow waters. Each year there are fifty to seventy confirmed shark attacks and five to fifteen shark-attack fatalities around the world, according to the International Shark Attack File. And in Africa, Australia, and the island nations of Southeast Asia, crocodile attacks are frighteningly common, because several species indigenous to these regions can survive comfortably in both freshwater and saltwater habitats. Estimates have placed the number of people killed by crocodiles in these regions at upward of 1,200 per year.

Related Images: Animals (p. 21); Chased, Being (p. 48); Monsters (p. 160); Paralysis/Running in Slow Motion (p. 178)

6. **ANIMALS**

Common
Manifestations:
It's like a marathon of the Animal Planet channel inside your dreaming mind. Perhaps you are at the local zoo, or even on safari, observing exotic animals in their natural settings. Or, you may just be dreaming of an encounter in the wild, whether that interaction is gentle, illuminating, or frightening. It's also possible that your dream centers on a pet. The common thread is the animal presence and your reaction to it.

Variations: In a disturbing variation of this dream, you are being
               attacked by a wild animal (p. 17).

Occurrence: Ominous animal dreams, similar to dreams of monsters
               hiding in the closet (p. 160), are extremely common
               in childhood, although they can recur in adulthood as
               well. Some studies have indicated that wild animal
               dreams are more common in male children than
               female children.

The Spin: As mentioned elsewhere, animals are obvious
               metaphors for the unconscious urges inside all of
               us—and the wilder the dream animal, the more base
               the urge. The habitual appearance of specific animals
               in your dreams might hint at deeper symbolism, but
               the type of animal in the dream is perhaps less signifi-
               cant than the behavior it exhibits. Dream expert Gayle
               Delaney recommends taking a moment to consider
               the personality and behavior of the animal. Did it
               appear with deadly stealth out of nowhere, or stomp
               and growl, announcing itself from afar? Was it possi-
               ble to communicate with the animal, or was it not
               responsive? Asking these questions might help you
               equate the dream behavior with a certain person or a
               similar experience you're having in waking life.

                   Specific animals can prompt latent images. Bears
               are ferocious creatures with great potential power that
               live out a kind of cyclical transformation every year—
               winter hibernation and spring awakening. Your opinion

of cats (sensual snugglebunny or nuisance?) and dogs (unconditional love or slobbering ball of energy?) might well depend on your childhood experiences, and whether you encountered them as pets. Elephants have an unsurpassed power and nobility, but get on their wrong side and they will flatten everything in sight. Ravens have long symbolized the inexorability of death (consider Poe's famous poem, and the continued presence, for hundreds of years, of a group of ravens at the Tower of London, a one-time prison and execution site). Snakes have a polarizing effect on people: Some view them as sources of higher consciousness and wisdom, creatures that continually reinvent themselves (in shedding their skin), while others view them as the embodiment of deceit and covert betrayal ("a snake in the grass").

What Freud Would Say:	For Freud, the dream of being pursued or threatened by animals usually pointed to a dreamer afraid of repressed passionate impulses. In fact, the wild beast itself represented a person consumed by those uncontrollable urges. Freud speculated that the wild animal could symbolize the libido and its untapped power; or that a dreamer might compartmentalize his neurosis or desire and, in the dream, turn it into a different creature to disassociate and alleviate anxiety.
What Jung Would Say:	Jung wrote at great length about animals, each with its own mythic and cultural symbolism. As

a phenomenon, however, he considered them dream archetypes of the Shadow self—symbols of the mysteries of the unconscious mind, or what he called the "dark center." Dream dictionary author Sandra Thomson makes the point that animals who talk or impart wisdom in your dream are archetypes for the Self or the Wise Old Man.

Related Images: Chased, Being (p. 48); Insects (p. 145); Monsters (p. 160); Paralysis/Running in Slow Motion (p. 178)

---

7. **ATTIC**

Common
Manifestations:
You're in a house you may or may not recognize, and you ascend a stairway that leads to the top floor and the attic. It may be a lifeless, dark room, or you may enter to find a treasure trove of photos, memorabilia, and furniture from several generations of your past. The attic might also be haunted by a spirit presence.

The Spin:

The house is a very personal, immediate dream symbol, one that can evoke a specific time in someone's life, but which can also serve as a metaphor for the self. Particular rooms of a house, and the function of those rooms, often reflect a particular aspect of the dreamer's personality. Unlike the basement, where you usually house things you want out of the way, the attic is, in waking life, often a repository of items that hold great sentimental value—old wedding dresses, antique furniture, or precious photos and diaries. So the attic could serve as a metaphor for the memories and traditions that have—however implicitly—shaped your life and your psyche. Some psychologists argue that the dream attic represents a body's intellect, or higher consciousness: An attic sits at the top of the house, just as the head sits atop the body. If ghosts dwell in your dream attic, perhaps you are preoccupied with events from your past, or you have not yet put to rest issues with a deceased loved one.

If Recurrent: Maybe it's time for a thorough spring cleaning, followed by a garage sale.

What Freud Would Say: Freud did not address dreams of attics per se. In *The Interpretation of Dreams*, he stated, "Rooms in dreams are usually women; if the various ways in and out of them are represented, this interpretation is scarcely open to doubt." Many dream interpreters who follow Freud have argued that just as the basement can be a metaphor for the unconscious mind, so can the attic be a symbol of the superego.

What Jung Would Say: The house is a metaphor for the Self—Jung famously referred to the house as the "mansion of the soul." Through dreaming, you will learn about aspects of the Self that you have previously repressed or obscured. Ascending the steps to your dream attic represents a willingness to explore your psyche; Jung says, in his book *Dreams*, that "the steps and ladders theme points to the process of psychic transformation, with all its ups and downs."

Related Images: Basement (p. 26); Corridors/Hallways (p. 64); Home, Childhood (p. 136); Kitchen (p. 151); Rooms, Secret (p. 199); Rooms, Unused (p. 202)

8.   **BASEMENT**

Common
Manifestations: You're in a house that may or may not be familiar to you, and you open a door to a stairway that goes down into a dark basement. You might be excited to explore the contents of the basement, especially if it's a house from your childhood (p. 136). But basement dreams can often be scary—the basement door is sometimes locked, or you are forbidden to go "down there."

The Spin: The house is a very personal, immediate dream symbol, one which can evoke a specific time in someone's life, but which can also serve as a metaphor for the self. Particular rooms of a house, and the function of those rooms, often reflect a particular aspect of the dreamer's personality. In waking life, the basement is the foundation of the house and the place where you store the unused detritus of your life—things you don't want visible in your home, or items you have forgotten about but are not yet willing to part with. Many psychologists equate the basement with the "base" notions of your unconscious mind, a repository for uncomfortable thoughts and urges that you don't want to see the light of day. Dream analyst Gillian Holloway calls the dream basement a "psychological space" where we file information and experiences still to be processed, which may one day be of use.

What Freud Would Say:

In *The Interpretation of Dreams*, Freud stated, "Rooms in dreams are usually women; if the various ways in and out of them are represented, this interpretation is scarcely open to doubt." The dream image of the basement representing the dark, intimidating unconscious is a classic Freudian symbol.

What Jung Would Say:

The house is a metaphor for the Self. Through dreaming, you will learn about aspects of the Self that you have previously repressed or obscured. Jung shared Freud's view that images of the basement represented the unconscious mind. If, in the dream, you're afraid to go into the basement, it could mean that you're unwilling to delve into the deeper recesses of your mind.

Cultural Context:

Basement imagery doesn't get any more Freudian than in Alfred Hitchcock's 1960 thriller *Psycho*. Contemplate the repressed Oedipal sexuality of Norman Bates living "with" his dead mother in the house adjacent to his motel. Midway through the film, he moves her corpse from her bedroom into the basement fruit cellar, where he can keep her hidden from authorities—the basement here reflecting Norman's twisted unconscious. By the end of the movie, the dark secret of Mrs. Bates is revealed, and she looms so large that, in a kind of a reverse Oedipal development, she takes over Norman's personality completely.

Related Images: Attic (p. 24); Corridors/Hallways (p. 64); Home, Childhood (p. 136); Kitchen (p. 151); Rooms, Secret (p. 199); Rooms, Unused (p. 202)

9.   **BEACH/OCEAN**

Common
Manifestations: You are walking along a beach, as salt water ebbs and flows over your feet. The crashing of waves is audible. It could be a hot summer day or even off-season.

Variations: This type of dream can have an ominous side as well. The water may overwhelm you; you may be sucked under in a riptide, in danger of drowning (p. 84); or violent waves may crash inexorably on shore—a storm surge that threatens you or perhaps your home.

Occurrence: This dream could have a very straightforward physiological prompt—you might simply be thirsty, or a full bladder could be sending a not-so-subliminal message that you need to use the facilities. A dream of a stormy ocean might reflect a fear of water, or a posttraumatic reenactment of a shipwreck or swimming accident.

The Spin:

Water is a potent dream symbol, one that evokes deep, often obscured emotions and can recall the amniotic fluid of a mother's womb. Deep bodies of water symbolize the unconscious—powerful, diverse, and largely hidden from view. The state of the water in your dream (crystalline, calm, stormy, littered with detritus) could provide clues to your underlying emotions. If the water in your dream turns ominous or life-threatening—and if you are not having a posttraumatic reaction to a real-life disaster—your waking-life emotions are likely highly volatile and potentially overwhelming. The sensation of struggling against—and being defeated by—a powerful force of nature is an apt metaphor for how overwhelmed you can feel by your emotions or by a seemingly intractable situation. Think about how a tsunami, associated with the unforgiving ocean and underwater earthquakes, could sweep you away suddenly, without warning.

???

Beaches, on the other hand, have interesting metaphoric connotations. They're transition environments where sand, associated with dry, hostile desert climates, meets the ocean, a mysterious, powerful entity that harbors thousands of creatures in its depths. In this case, the sand disappearing into the water could symbolize the tension between the known (terra firma) and the unknown (the unseen deep). If the ocean seems welcoming in the dream, your mind may be signaling its willingness to explore your unconscious realms. If, however, you stand on the shore and watch the waves crash violently at your feet, perhaps you're frightened at the prospect of finding out what lies in the depths of your mind—that once you dive in, so to speak, you might be sucked under, unable to return to the safety of that which you know.

If Recurrent:	Maybe you just *really* need a vacation. Listen to your unconscious, and pack a towel and some sunscreen.
What Freud Would Say:	In *The Interpretation of Dreams*, Freud argued that water images evoked memories of the womb and birth and regressive thoughts of childhood. Dreams in which the water, in whatever form, turned sinister could indicate anxiety about sex and repression of forbidden thoughts of bed-wetting.
What Jung Would Say:	Water is often representative of feminine energy (the Anima), and symbolizes the mystery of the unconscious. Large or powerful bodies of water are archetypal symbols for the collective unconscious. Men who fear water in real life may harbor fears of women, or of their emotional/feminine side.

Cultural
Context:

Metaphorically speaking, the ocean symbolizes the great, mysterious unknown—a description that carries over to the scientific realm as well. In 2000, the Smithsonian Institution of Washington, D.C., commissioned a Census of Marine Life to identify and catalog the more than 210,000 known marine life-forms, but scientists involved in the project estimate that the actual number of life-forms could be up to ten times higher. Though astonishingly biodiverse, as an environment, the ocean is hostile to human life: We cannot breathe underwater (p. 84), nor can we ingest saltwater for hydration. Evolution theory states that life began in the Earth's oceans and continued as such until sometime during the Devonian period, 390 million years ago, when man's primordial ancestors, the first amphibians, developed lungs, grew legs, and crawled from the ocean.

Related Images: Desert Island (p. 81); Drowning/Breathing Underwater (p. 84); Natural Disasters: Earthquakes, Hurricanes, Tornadoes, and Volcanoes (p. 172); Water (p. 230)

10.   ## BED, SOMETHING UNDER

Common
Manifestations:

It's bedtime. You turn off the light to go to sleep, but have the disturbing sense that something savage lurks unseen in the dark, under the bed, waiting to attack until you are asleep, at your most vulnerable. You wake with a start, convinced that you hear another set of lungs breathing, or see a pair of eyes glowing in the blackness. Good luck getting back to sleep after *that* dream.

Variations: Monsters hiding in the closet is another popular manifestation of this dream (p. 160).

Occurrence: Children report having this dream more than any other.

The Spin: In the simplest terms, this dream gives voice to a child's fear of the unknown. Times of change and upheaval can be traumatizing, even if change brings something good. Starting a new school, welcoming a baby sibling, or overhearing a fight between parents can introduce feelings of instability and uncertainty to the environment. It's a time when a child's horizons are expanding exponentially—interacting with other kids and adults, assuming small responsibilities at school and home, even taking the first steps in learning about the scary world of sex (hence the goblins hiding under the bed, specifically). These events converge and leave a kid feeling as if life is not within her control. Who knows what other scary stuff is hiding out there, where you can't see it?

If Recurrent: Try to stay in a routine and minimize upheaval in the child's life. Creating an environment in which the child feels secure and stable will go a long way toward banishing these dreams.

What Freud Would Say:	Monsters or other beasts that appear in dreams usually represent repressed urges that scare or intimidate the dreamer. Freud speculated, not surprisingly, that the beast symbolized sexual aggression and power (a beast hiding under the bed drives that point home even more forcefully). He also believed that the dreamer turns this repressed urge into an entirely different creature in order to disassociate from it and alleviate the anxiety that such feelings cause.
What Jung Would Say:	The bed—a place where your mind and body lie to rest and you enter the world of dreams—can be interpreted as the portal between your conscious and unconscious realms, according to the Jungian dream analysis Web site mythsdreamssymbols.com. Worrying about monsters under the bed is a likely indication that something powerful in your unconscious is pushing its way to the surface, demanding to be reckoned with.
Cultural Context:	These types of dreams evoke a kind of visceral fear that the places where we are the safest—our home, our bed—are really not so safe at all. The Brothers Grimm exploited these very fears; their fairy tales, though intended for children, depicted the world as a heartless, capricious, and violent place. In the Grimm universe, children are stalked by creatures hiding in a bed (Little Red Riding Hood), repeatedly attacked by jealous family members (Snow White), and abandoned

by their parents to the mercies of a child-eating witch
(Hansel and Gretel).

Related Images: Aliens (p. 13); Chased, Being (p. 48); Monsters
(p. 160); Paralysis/Running in Slow Motion (p. 178)

---

11.   **BIBLICAL FIGURES AND RELIGIOUS ICONS**

Common
Manifestations:
You are visited in your dream by a divine icon, be
it Mary, Muhammad, Moses, Jesus, or Buddha. The
apparition packs a powerful wallop, and you are
struck mute with love and humility. After a moment's
recovery, you may start peppering questions at your
dream prophet (what is the meaning of life? etc.), or
you may simply keep silent as you wait to receive an
important message. As with a similar dream of visitation from angels (p. 16), you wake feeling blessed and
profoundly moved.

The Spin:
Dreams of prophets, saints, and saviors can have a
transformative impact, whether you perceive the visitation to be an authentic spiritual vision or simply a
powerful, positive metaphor. Visions of a higher
power or deity are usually dreams that invite epiphany.
In some cases the divine dream figure could represent
the dreamer's higher, nobler consciousness, imparting
a wisdom that the dreamer is only now ready to accept.

If Recurrent:	What, you didn't hear your personalized, divine message the first time? Take heed, already!
What Freud Would Say:	Freud, an atheist, believed all religion to be an illusion, a form of cultural neurosis resulting from childhood or primitive guilt over the Oedipus complex.
What Jung Would Say:	Jung had strong personal faith and believed that religion helped to bring a person in touch with the archetypes and traditions of the collective unconscious. In Jung's world of archetypes, images of male gods in women's dreams most likely represented the Animus, and images of female gods in men's dreams often represented the Anima. The Virgin Mary was a version of the Great Mother, a symbol of love, sex, and motherhood. And Jung sees in Jesus Christ's death and resurrection a beautiful allusion to the ways in which the psyche continues to reinvent itself on the journey toward individuation, as old ways of thinking die off and new, higher insights are brought to life.
Cultural Context:	Receiving a religious vision isn't always what it's cracked up to be. This highly personal, life-changing event can be confusing, and telling others about it is likely to invite ridicule and even condemnation. Joan of Arc learned this lesson all too well. The fifteenth-century French teenager received visions from several Catholic saints, urging her to lead French forces in driving the English out of France. Dressed in men's

clothes, she proved a savvy military strategist despite her youth and inexperience, but shortly after the French secured victory, she was captured by the British, tried, and burned at the stake for heresy.

Related Images: Angels (p. 16); End of the World (p. 98); Historical Figures (p. 134)

---

12.   **BOAT**

Common Manifestations: You are traveling in a boat across a body of water. The boat itself could be an intimate two-person craft or a full-size cruise liner. The length of the trip could be epic or incidental, the conditions smooth, speedy, or turbulent. The tenor of your voyage depends much on your state of mind at the time of the dream.

Variations: A more ominous version of this dream is one in which your boat begins to sink or you are in danger of a shipwreck (p. 8).

The Spin: In dreams, modes of transportation often have enormous personal significance; different vehicles may symbolize a love relationship, your body, your personal autonomy, even your life as a whole. According to dream dictionary author Sandra Thomson, boats symbolize the relationship between your conscious and unconscious minds, and long sailing trips can represent the exploration of the unconscious realm. Reflect on the type of boat in your dream: Is it a rickety rowboat buffeted by the currents, a sleek catamaran that speeds across the surface of the waves, or a formidable mega-ship that resembles a floating metropolis? Are you the ship's captain, or do you sit to one side and allow someone else to chart the course? Assessing your role in this dream voyage could shed light on how you take charge of (or abdicate) responsibility for your own feelings. On the flip side, problems with your dream ship could point to challenges you face in coping with stress and emotional trauma, or perhaps a resistance to plumbing your own unconscious depths.

If Recurrent:	Cruise lines offer great discounts this time of year.
What Freud Would Say:	Freud believed that ships and "vessels of all kinds" were dream symbols for the uterus.
What Jung Would Say:	In *Dreams*, Jung analyzed several transportation-related dreams: "The type of vehicle in a dream illustrates the kind of movement or the manner in which the dreamer moves forward in time—in other words, how he lives his psychic life, whether individually or collectively, whether on his own or on borrowed means, whether spontaneously or mechanically." For Jung, water represented feminine energy (the Anima) and symbolized the mystery of the unconscious. Large or powerful bodies of water were

archetypal symbols for the collective unconscious, and traveling by boat across oceans and seas was a metaphoric exercise in self-discovery. The larger the ship, the more the craft served as a metaphor for the journey toward individuation.

Cultural Context:

Boats were perhaps the first man-made forms of transportation, propelled by wind or oars. Recorded history shows that technological and material limitations did not prevent early civilizations from imagining a world beyond their borders and sailing large swaths of the planet's oceans. Perhaps the earliest active ocean explorers were the Phoenicians, circa 500 BCE, who sailed and traded from the English Channel all the way east to the Indian Ocean. In modern times, Norwegian explorer and writer Thor Heyerdahl set out to prove, in a 1947 expedition, that it was possible for the indigenous peoples of South America to have settled in Polynesia, all the way across the Pacific Ocean, during pre-Columbian times. His team built a balsawood raft, christened the *Kon-Tiki*, using only the methods and materials that would have been available at the time, and made the more than 4,300-mile (6,900 km) trip from Peru to the Tuamotu Islands in 101 days.

Related Images:

Accident with Airplane, Train, Car, or Boat (p. 8); Beach/Ocean (p. 28); Desert Island (p. 81)

13. **BRAIN**

Common
Manifestations:

Most dreams that relate specifically to the brain are framed in the language of anxiety and nightmare. A monster may try to eat your brain, or some powerful outside force may have taken control of your brain. Perhaps you have suddenly discovered, to your consternation, a foreign object or weapon embedded in your frontal lobe. Or, you may dream of having an incurable brain ailment.

Occurrence:

These types of dreams often arise when you are feeling stifled, frustrated, or unable to think clearly.

The Spin:

As the repository of intellect, memory, and consciousness, the brain is often a central feature in problem-solving dreams. If you dream of something consuming or commandeering your brain, you may feel that a person or institution in your life (perhaps a boss, a course of study, or a lover) is squelching your true abilities and talents. In the same way, dreaming of a brain illness could simply indicate that someone in your waking life is being a real pain in the neck, as it were. Dreams of surgically removing a strange object from your brain, on the other hand, often have more positive connotations—they indicate that you have been able to free yourself of a mental block or psychological obstacle that, until now, has held you back.

If Recurrent:	Pinpoint your brain's role in your dream—automaton? diseased organ? or host of an alien object?—and then assess whether that evokes a similar situation in your waking life.
What Freud Would Say:	Freud rejected the notion that dreams carry problem-solving functions—not surprising, since it contradicts his central assumption: that dreams represent the assertion of purely unconscious wishes. In *The Interpretation of Dreams*, he stated that "thinking ahead, forming intentions, framing attempted solutions" merely "persist in the state of sleep as 'the day's residues,'" and are often merged with an unrelated, unconscious wish-fulfillment to form a dream.
What Jung Would Say:	Speaking of the world of collective myths and dream images, Jung called the skull "the first spherical form," stating, "According to tradition, the head or brain is the seat of the *Anima intellectualis* [intellectual spirit]."
Cultural Context:	Although today we usually consider the life lessons gleaned from dreams to be the interpret-them-yourself variety, the notion that dreams can provide problem-solving insight dates back to the ancient Egyptians and Greeks. The Egyptians believed that all dreams were messages from the gods, intended to warn of future danger, answer questions, or chastise immoral or impious behavior. Dream temples, called *serapea*, honored several Egyptian gods, including Bes

(said to deliver happy dreams and ward off evil spirits during sleep) and Imhotep (god of healing). Interpreters who lived in the temples helped supplicants understand the meanings of their dreams. Similarly, Greek dream temples honored Aesculapius, the god of healing. A Greek seeking guidance hoped for an "invitation" (in a dream) to visit the temple; once there, he would practice "incubation"—offering a gift or animal sacrifice and sleeping in the temple, for multiple nights if necessary—until Aesculapius or one of his attendants granted a visit to help solve his waking-life problem. The speed of response was thought to be directly related to one's social standing: The dreams of the upper class and royalty, for example, were said to be answered the fastest.

Related Images: Hair (p. 129); Mouth and Teeth (p. 166); Teeth Falling Out (p. 219)

14.   **CAR TROUBLE/DRIVING PROBLEMS**

Common Manifestations: You are driving down the road when it becomes clear that your car is having problems. Perhaps the brakes fail, the radiator overheats, you run out of gas, or you get a flat tire. In a more dire scenario, the car spins out of control. Having an accident (p. 8) is a real possibility.

Occurrence:	This dream might arise as a mild posttraumatic remembrance of a recent car accident.
The Spin: ??? ♡	In dreams, modes of transportation often have enormous personal significance; different vehicles may symbolize different relationships, your own body, or even your life as a whole. Cars, often omnipresent in everyday life, can symbolize the physical body and how you move through life. Are you driving the vehicle, or is someone you know taking you for a ride? Is the car hurtling out of control, or traveling sedately along on a Sunday drive? If your dream car needs repairing, remember that the specific type of car trouble can have metaphoric implications. If the brakes fail, perhaps you feel as if you're losing control of an important life situation. An overheated radiator? Maybe you've blown your top recently and need to get your temper back under control. Running out of gas may be a gentle admonishment to rest and recharge before you burn yourself out.
If Recurrent:	Have you changed the oil lately?
What Freud Would Say:	Similar to dreams of missing a train (p. 61), which Freud believed were anxiety dreams about the fear of death, dreams of dangerous driving or vehicular crashes could easily be interpreted as an expression of Thanatos, or the death wish.

What Jung Would Say:	In his book *Dreams*, Jung argued that the type of vehicle that appears in a transportation-related dream was directly related to the way a person approaches life. Jung finds significance in whether the method of transportation is individual or collective, self-propelled or mechanical.
Cultural Context:	Cars are regarded differently in various cultures. Americans, for example, may be thought to overly identify with their cars, seeing them as necessary accessories. In many areas of the United States, this is the case, as suburban sprawl requires traveling significant distances in one's daily life. In other countries, however, cars hold no particular personal significance. They may indicate wealth or luxury, however—those who can afford to have a car have disposable income.
Related Images:	Accident with Airplane, Train, Car, or Boat (p. 8); Connections, Missed (p. 61); Vehicle That Isn't a Vehicle (p. 226)

15. **CAVE**

Common Manifestations:	You find yourself in a cave—dark, damp, and cool. The way out is unclear, and illumination may be hard to come by. The passages twist, turn, and fork as you feel your way along the walls, searching for a path to follow. You may move toward a dim light that leads

you to the surface, or you may venture deeper into the cave, stumbling upon a hidden treasure or a secret chamber of unsurpassed, ethereal beauty.

The Spin: Caves are dark, protected areas, representing a haven from the stresses and concerns seen in the harsh light of day. As such, they often symbolize a desire to return to the safety and protection of the womb. This might be a message from your unconscious mind that it's time to take a mental-health break and recharge your emotional batteries.

Caves can also represent the mysteries of the unconscious mind. Once you enter a cave, it's hard to see where you are going, and without a guide (or some form of illumination), you remain blind to much of what lies within. Making your way through the maze-like passages of a cave is an evocative illustration of the unforeseen detours and wrong turns you take on a journey toward self-discovery. If, in the dream, you worry that the dark cave harbors dangerous animals, you might fear what revelations await in your unconscious mind. On the other hand, dreaming that you have found your way out of a cave—or even traveling so far inside to have discovered a hidden chamber full of beauty or treasure—could indicate you've reached an epiphany that will change your life.

If Recurrent: You might have an unconscious desire to try your hand at spelunking.

What Freud Would Say:	As dark places to enter or leave, with light shining through the opening, caves are, along with tunnels, classic Freudian symbols for the vagina.
What Jung Would Say:	For Jung, the cave represented "the darkness and seclusion of the unconscious"—a place that, when explored, can lead to greater self-knowledge.
Cultural Context:	Jung's notion of the cave as metaphor for the unconscious has its origins in Plato's seminal philosophical work, *The Republic*. In it, he relates the Parable of the Cave, which illustrates his view of the known and unknown worlds. Plato tells the story of a group of prisoners who have spent their entire lives chained inside a cave, facing a wall. Behind the prisoners is a fire that burns constantly, as free people walk to and fro, attending their business. The shadows of the free people are cast upon the cave wall, and the prisoners grow to believe that this shadow world represents true reality—never knowing what goes on behind them, in the world of actual forms. Were a prisoner to break free of his chains and turn around, he would no doubt be blinded by the firelight, unable to process or understand the "unreal" shapes before him. This allegory can therefore be interpreted on the personal level, as a metaphor for Jung's individuation process (the exploration of the obscured unconscious in search of the "true" self), as well as on the universal level,

in humanity's collective, never-ending search for a
higher purpose behind its existence.

Related Images: Lost, Being (p. 155); Mud (p. 169); Treasure, Buried
(p. 222); Tunnel (p. 225)

16.   **CELEBRITIES**

Common
Manifestations:

Talk about an affair to remember. In this dream,
you're hobnobbing with the rich and famous. You
might be attending a get-together of A-listers, at
which you're the life of the party. Or it could be a
steamier, one-on-one encounter with your favorite
celebrity fantasy. The quality of the dream may vary
from the quotidian (you invite Madonna to your son's
soccer tournament, and she shows up with snacks) to
the bizarre (you are riding cross-country on the back
of a motorcycle with Jon Bon Jovi). The salient feature
is the presence of someone ripped from the pages of
People magazine.

The Spin:

To dream of celebrities is to dream of mythic ideals.
Focus on the personality traits of the celebrity in your
dream—is it someone charming? Funny? Good-hearted?
Highly sexual? Then think about how you interacted
with this person. Was your stature elevated by this
celebrity's presence? Did the charm, humor, or sex
appeal rub off with your proximity? Your unconscious

mind could be highlighting a desire for fame. Or, often, the characteristics you ascribe to a celebrity—however misplaced—are ones you'd like to assume yourself. Pinpoint what a particular celebrity means to you, and you'll go a long way toward decoding the dream image.

If Recurrent: You may be destined for your own reality TV show.

What Freud Would Say: Freud analyzed dreams of and about well-known historical persons, but didn't ascribe a meaning to the characters in the dream—only the content.

What Jung Would Say: According to the Jungian dream analysis Web site mythsdreamssymbols.com, famous people who turn up in dreams often represent qualities to which you aspire, or qualities in your personality that you have not yet acknowledged in your conscious mind. In this way, the dream celebrity may correspond to your Shadow archetype or may represent particular aspects of your Persona.

Cultural Context:

There's a fine line between dreaming of your favorite celebrity and fixating on a remote embodiment of some psychic ideal. John Hinckley Jr. tried to assassinate then-president Ronald Reagan in 1981 because of his obsession with the actress Jodie Foster. Hinckley had repeatedly watched the movie *Taxi Driver*, in which Foster played a teen prostitute and Robert De Niro, the taxi driver in question, plotted to assassinate a presidential candidate.

Related Images: Biblical Figures and Religious Icons (p. 34); Historical Figures (p. 134)

17.   **CHASED, BEING**

Common
Manifestations: Someone dangerous chases you; it could be a wild animal, a faceless figure (or figures), a threatening person in your life, or even a monster or alien. You don't remember what precipitated the chase—it's as if you joined a dream already in progress. You feel the pursuer gain on you, and no matter what super-human or fantastic steps you take to escape, you can't seem to make it go away. A sense of helplessness and inevitability overwhelms you, and (usually before getting caught) you wake up shaken, with your heart pounding.

Variations: You try as hard as you can to elude capture, but you are running in slow motion, or feel paralyzed and can't seem to get away (p. 178).

Occurrence: Along with falling dreams, dreams of being chased are probably the most commonly experienced in the world—one that occurs for people across all cultural, historical, ethnic, and educational backgrounds. This dream usually begins in childhood, with the familiar dream of being chased by monsters (p. 160) or wild animals (p. 21).

The Spin: You're avoiding something. Maybe it's a stressful situation in your life, or a decision you're not ready to make. You could be harboring feelings or personality traits that scare you. The fact that your fictive pursuer is relentless should be an obvious sign that you can't outrun the problem. But if the thing chasing you appears faceless or hulkingly amorphous, how should you tackle the fear? Dream expert Gayle Delaney recommends asking some questions. What will the pursuer do if you are caught? What does he/she/it want? Try to describe the personality of the person or thing that chases you—and then see if that description matches your feelings about a problem or situation in your life.

If Recurrent: Chase dreams recur at different stages of everyone's life. However, if the same dream pursuer hounds you multiple times, it's time to practice your lucid dreaming skills. While dreaming, should you have the presence of mind to stop running, turn around, and confront the entity chasing you ("Why are you chasing me? What do you want?"), the answer might surprise you. Numerous psychologists have reported that dreamers who find a way to control the chase in their dream often have long, illuminating conversations with the person or thing chasing them. Once you know what pursues you and why, the dream rarely recurs.

What Freud
Would Say:

Freud will be Freud. For him, dreams of being chased actually indicated an unconscious sexual wish—the dreamer might run away, but really wants to be caught and ravished. Psychologist and dream analyst Sandra Thomson notes the possible play on words between *chaste* and *chased*.

What Jung
Would Say:

Jung might have categorized this as a "remembered" dream, one from the collective unconscious that recalls more primitive societies in which man was hunted or pursued by wild animals. Or, he might have considered the chase more symbolic; you flee a part of your psyche— perhaps the Shadow archetype, your "dark side"— that makes you uncomfortable or that you don't want to acknowledge. Jung placed great stock in balance and self-acceptance, and would consider the work of identifying your pursuer and confronting your fear very significant.

Cultural
Context:

The person or thing who chases—relentless, threatening, indestructible—has been the centerpiece of an entire genre of fiction, film, and television. But the most riveting portrayal of the living nightmare that is a never-ending chase would have to be the 1960s television drama *The Fugitive* (remade as a 1993 blockbuster starring Harrison Ford and Tommy Lee Jones). David

Janssen played the TV version of Dr. Richard Kimble, an innocent man convicted of murdering his wife. He escaped police custody on the way to jail, and, for four seasons, stayed on the run, searching for the one-armed man who killed his wife. (Lt. Philip Gerard, the marshal who relentlessly hunts Kimble, won't help him and doesn't believe his story—a classic aspect of the chase dream.) In the 1967 series finale, "The Judgment" (at the time, the highest-rated episode in the history of television), Dr. Kimble finally found his one-armed man, who confessed to the murder. It was, in the words of the show's narrator, "the day the running stopped."

Related Images: Crime, Victim of (p. 70); Monsters (p. 160); Paralysis/Running in Slow Motion (p. 178)

---

18. **CHILD, FORGETTING OR MISPLACING**

Common
Manifestations:
You are living through the ordinary routine of your day when you find, hidden in a closet or unused room, a crying baby. You discover, to your horror, that the child is your responsibility (although the child does not correspond to an actual waking-life son or daughter), and you have left it untended for weeks, months, even years. Feelings of shame and guilt over-whelm you.

Variations: In a similar dream, you have left your toddler or young
                child somewhere—in the car, store, or restaurant—as
                you rush around to complete an endless list of
                responsibilities under a time crunch.

Occurrence: This type of dream, strangely, often appears to middle-
♀ ⅰ ⅰ   aged women who have no children or older women
                who have adult children.

The Spin: The obvious interpretation—that you're worried
???   about being a good parent—is rarely the accurate
                one. More often, the dream baby represents a part of
                yourself, a deeply felt hope or wish that you've over-
                looked or neglected for too long. Perhaps it's not that
                you have taken the wrong life path, but that you have
                compromised on something that's more important to
                you than you realize.

                Dreaming that you've dumped the kids somewhere
                in order to execute your never-ending errands, on the
                other hand, is probably an exaggerated expression of
                how overwhelmed you feel with the responsibilities in
                your life.

If Recurrent: Your unconscious is asking you to pay attention.
                Take a step back and look at the big picture. How
                did you feel in the dream when you discovered the
                unattended baby? Does thinking about a goal or
                desire that you have cherished and yet abandoned
                evoke the same feelings?

What Jung Would Say:	The baby in your dream is most likely a hidden or unknown aspect of your personality, one that remains a mystery to you. And instead of paying attention to the parts of your psyche that need care and feeding, you've "forgotten" about them (the way you "forgot" about the baby in your dream), and in doing so have missed out on a chance to learn more about yourself.
Cultural Context:	The notion of a lost or missing child evokes an elemental fear in adults. Interestingly, this fear is cultivated in many classic works of children's literature, including *The Wonderful Wizard of Oz*, *Alice's Adventures in Wonderland*, and multiple entries in the Brothers Grimm's dark, brutal fairy tales. But perhaps the most shocking and lurid real-life incident in the last hundred years was the kidnapping of Charles Lindbergh's infant son, Charles Jr., from the family home in East Amwell, New Jersey, in 1932.
Related Images:	Lost, Being (p. 155); Purse or Wallet, Lost (p. 193)

---

19. **CITY**

Common Manifestations:	You find yourself in the middle of a large, thriving city. Perhaps you stride down the busy streets with purpose, a definite destination in mind. Or maybe you meander, stopping to investigate whatever interests you. However you explore this city, the salient features of

the dream are the crowded, close-in buildings and the vast sense of place and potential the city has to offer.

Variations: This dream could have ominous overtones: You may be lost in a dangerous neighborhood or surrounded by unfriendly residents.

The Spin: Just as different rooms of a house can symbolize
🔦 ??? different aspects of the dreamer's personality, so can different city neighborhoods (or even individual buildings in a city) represent specific personality traits. Dream dictionary author Sandra Thomson takes this analogy in a fascinating direction: To be at home and familiar in a dream city, she says, is to know the ins and outs of your personality—the high-brow, cultural parts as well as the dark, dangerous parts. The ease in which you navigate the city of your dreams could correspond to the extent of your self-knowledge: Is your dream city laid out in an organized grid, with easy-to-find addresses and large public squares? Or do the roads twist and turn, circling back on each other, until you find yourself hopelessly lost?

What Freud The tall, pointy skyscraper that soars into the sky is a
Would Say: classic Freudian phallic symbol.

What Jung For Jung, a city—especially a fortified, walled city or
Would Say: courtyard—represented the Self.

Cultural Context:	The city as metaphor for the self is a concept almost as old as civilization itself. *Metropolis* is a Greek word meaning, literally, "mother city." In ancient Greece, the word was used to denote a parent state that other satellite societies turned to for guidance.
Related Images:	Attic (p. 24); Basement (p. 26); Corridors/Hallways (p. 64); Home, Childhood (p. 136); Kitchen (p. 151); Mother (p. 163); Rooms, Secret (p. 199); Rooms, Unused (p. 202)

20. 📷 **COMMUNICATION BREAKDOWN**

Common Manifestations:	You're in a crisis and need help—perhaps you're lost, or your car has broken down, or you need medical treatment. You try to call for help, but your phone is dead or your cell phone doesn't get service. Or you call for emergency services and no one picks up. If someone does answer, the person is uncooperative to the point of rudeness. You wake up anxious and frustrated.
Variations:	A similar dream deals with spoken-word barriers. When you ask for help, you realize that everyone around you speaks an unfamiliar language, and you can't make yourself understood. Or conversely, when you try to speak, all that comes out is gibberish, and no one takes you seriously.

The Spin: The meaning here is pretty straightforward. You're
              having trouble being heard. Something important is on
              your mind—a message that needs communicating.
              But you are unable to effectively convey your concerns
              and fears. It might be your own inhibitions that jam
              the signal. Or the trouble you have "getting through"
              may be a commentary on the fractious relationship
              you have with the person you need to speak to.

              If, in the dream, you make the connection but are
              rebuffed or shooed away by an unsympathetic authority
              figure (an emergency services operator, a police officer,
              a doctor), then perhaps, in your waking life, you have
              been soliciting the wrong person for help or support.

If Recurrent: It could be time to look inward. Maybe the person
               who's not paying attention is you. Have you been
               ignoring a problem or putting off an uncomfortable
               decision because you just don't want to deal? This
               may be your unconscious telling you to get on with
               it, already.

What Freud   Freud believed that the unconscious was extremely
Would Say: deliberate in using language and symbols to illustrate
               a dream, choosing dialogue that employed hidden
               meanings, puns, and coded messages. This internal
               process extended to the work of the dream censor as
               well, which, under the powerful influence of repression,
               chose how the dream was remembered.

Cultural Context:	Astrologers believe that during times when the planet Mercury, considered a symbol of communication and intellect, is retrograde—meaning Earth's orbit is situated such that Mercury appears to be traveling backward in the sky—communications go awry and messages are misunderstood. It's difficult to pinpoint exactly how many distinct languages are spoken in the world, but most estimates place the figure at roughly five to six thousand. The most commonly spoken language in the world is Mandarin Chinese, with more than one billion native speakers. A small movement has lobbied for adopting Esperanto as a universal second language. Invented in 1887 by Dr. L. L. Zamenhof as a cross-cultural and culturally neutral tongue, Esperanto's grammar is structured with built-in flexibility that allows speakers from vastly different language groups to effectively translate their thoughts. Attempts to get Esperanto named the official language of the United Nations have so far been unsuccessful.
Related Images:	Connections, Missed (p. 61); Mechanical Malfunction (p. 158); Paralysis/Running in Slow Motion (p. 178)

21. 📷 **COMPUTERS**

Common Manifestations:	You're having computer troubles. A virus could be at fault, or the reason could be a mystery. You turn on the machine and try to execute the simplest task, but

nothing is working—maybe the screen goes blank or flashes with gibberish code. The keys could be scrambled on the keyboard, so you can't type a message. Any attempt to fix the problem or reboot just makes it worse; often, you feel stuck in a *Groundhog Day* loop, where you encounter the same error messages over and over, unable to make progress.

Variations: One variation is to dream that a computer has started to think for itself, acting independently of your wishes and commands. Following this image to its extreme, the dream computer might even take over your thought process and control your life.

Occurrence: Computer-frustration dreams often arise at times when you face a tough life decision, or when you're weighed down by stress.

The Spin: As purely algorithmic, analytic machines, computers
 are a lovely metaphor for logical, calculating, right-brain activity. So dreaming of a computer virus or malfunction could be symptomatic of a problem with your waking-life thought process. Have you been behaving irrationally? Are you clinging to an obsolete way of thinking, which is slowing down your ability to "process" information around you? Or do you continue to beat your head against a wall, reacting the exact same way to a problem that vexes you? This might be a sign that you need to take a step

back and start over ("reboot"), to change your approach to the situation.

On the other hand, dreaming of a computer that becomes autonomous or takes over your life could be a warning that you're being a little *too* Spocklike in your thinking. Dream dictionary author Sandra Thomson believes that computers in dreams carry the message that you're turning off emotions and operating on autopilot, ignoring the demands and desires of your heart.

If Recurrent:	You are wedded to a fixed way of thinking, and it's holding you back. Or perhaps you need to reacquaint yourself with *Computing for Dummies*.
What Freud Would Say:	Clearly Freud's life and work predate the computer as a presence in everyday life. However, Freud did address dreams of frustration, in which a task cannot be completed. He called these punishment dreams, which arise out of the mind's masochistic impulses. He felt these were most common at times when one's waking life was quite successful, another example of what he called dream reversals. In some cases, Freud also felt the inability to achieve a certain task, or dreams that involved broken-down machines, hinted at a fear of impotence.
What Jung Would Say:	For Jung, dreams of frustration often signified an emotional disturbance or conflict within the psyche—

between the conscious and unconscious minds, or between such opposing internal forces as masculine and feminine or aggression and passivity.

Cultural Context:

The notion that computers might one day technologically evolve into autonomous decision makers with the potential to take over one's life has rich metaphoric overtones ("I am a slave to the machines that make my life 'easier'") and ominous implications. One trailblazing work that tackles this question head-on is Stanley Kubrick's 1968 film *2001: A Space Odyssey*. The film has inspired critical essays on widely disparate topics; such a range of interpretation is understandable, given the film's minimal dialogue and often deliberate visual ambiguity. But it appears that one of Kubrick's primary hypotheses is that humankind can be dwarfed, and ultimately destroyed, by the very innovations that advance it. Arguably, the movie's central "character" is HAL 9000, the talking computer that controls the ship. In sharp contrast to the ship's astronauts, who move through each day like automatons, HAL expresses the "human" emotions of nervousness, concern, and curiosity. It is HAL that keeps the true nature of the mission a secret from the humans on the ship. And it's HAL who turns paranoid, murderous, and desperate after realizing that the astronauts want to take the computer offline and reclaim control of the ship. The power HAL wields in the film speaks to a type of omnipotent illogic commonly found in dream imagery.

Related Images: The Impossible Task (p. 140); Mechanical Malfunction
                    (p. 158)

22. 📷   **CONNECTIONS, MISSED**

Common   You're rushing to catch a plane, train, boat, or bus,
Manifestations: but something delays you—traffic, a forgotten
                engagement, a bureaucratic snafu. Despite the time
                crunch, you can't seem to circumvent the diversion.
                The clock ticks, and you become increasingly agitated
                at the thought of missing your departure. Often, a
                person or group of people corral you and insist on
                getting help before you leave, and you're either too
                polite, or feel too obligated, to refuse them. Or per-
                haps the need to be somewhere is only a nagging,
                peripheral sense of unease as you get caught up in
                some unrelated, frivolous endeavor—watching a
                sporting event, strolling through the park, or lounging
                in a café.

Variations: You're where you need to be, but the mode of trans-
                port is not. For example, you're standing in the train
                station, staring at the schedule board, unable to find
                your train and track number. Or you breeze through
                airport security, but when you get to the gate, a com-
                pletely different flight is boarding, and no one can tell
                you where your flight is. Sitting behind the wheel of a
                car, you may have traveled the same route a hundred

times before, but this time, you get hopelessly lost—
or you start on the correct highway but magically end
up on an unfamiliar road, with no idea how to get
back on track.

The Spin: The image of being late for an important journey
serves as a compelling metaphor for missed chances.
Dwelling on lost opportunities sparks a sharp frustration; something stands in the way of achieving one
of your goals—and that something could come from
within or without. If your dream self is busy solving
someone else's problems instead of getting to the airport, then maybe in real life, you need to stop putting
other people's needs before your own. But consider
the possibility that the root cause is your own anxiety.
If you dither with inconsequential details and never
seem to get around to the big decisions, such procras-
tination may indicate that you harbor ambivalence
about success. In the dream, if you make it to the
station but then can't find your train, maybe you're simply unsure of how to get what you want. With this
dream, your unconscious is prompting you to get off
your butt, take action, or get help. Bottom line: Don't
miss the boat.

A more straightforward interpretation is possible.
If your life is exceptionally busy, this dream might be
shouting the signal that your schedule is overloaded.
In that case, cut back on commitments and, occasionally, leave the PDA or day planner behind.

If Recurrent:	Get a good alarm clock, pack for your trip several nights before departing, and leave plenty of time to get to the airport.
What Freud Would Say:	Dreams of missing a train are directly related to fears of death. Leaving on a trip represents dying. So in missing the train, the dream actually offers comfort, consoling the dreamer that the bell has not yet tolled for him.
What Jung Would Say:	Dreams of rushing to catch a train symbolize the dreamer's journey toward self-realization. But Jung cautioned that such dreams could also hint at a neurosis for overachieving, especially as it relates to one's career. Dreams with boat imagery involve connecting with the Anima, or feminine energy within all of us. "Missing the boat" means you failed to take the opportunity to learn more about yourself.
Cultural Context:	Missed connections and lost opportunities are a staple feature of Hollywood fare, with such classic examples as Cary Grant and Deborah Kerr's thwarted Empire State Building rendezvous in *An Affair to Remember*. But it's hard to top the classic 1987 John Hughes comedy *Planes, Trains & Automobiles*, in which harried ad exec Steve Martin ping-pongs around the country, battling snow, flaming cars, and pathologically eager-to-please salesman John Candy ("Those aren't pillows") in his attempt to get home to Chicago in time for Thanksgiving dinner.

Related Images: Airplane (p. 11); Communication Breakdown
(p. 55); Mechanical Malfunction (p. 158)

23. 📷   **CORRIDORS/HALLWAYS**

Common
Manifestations: You are inside a house, walking down a hallway. It could
be a long hallway that, illogically, seems to stretch
into infinity, or it could be a maze of dead ends and
forked passages. You may see multiple doors along the
corridor, or you could be trapped in this "road to
nowhere," with no option but to move forward.

Variations: This type of dream may also involve staircases that
ascend or descend endlessly, with no landing in sight.

The Spin: The house is a very personal, immediate dream symbol.
💡 ???   Particular rooms of a house, and the function of those
rooms, often reflect a particular aspect of the dreamer's
personality. Passageways that have doors on either side
represent decisions to be made. The doors you see
could be the options in front of you, and conversely, a
long hallway with no doorways could indicate that
you have already chosen a path and must follow it
through to completion. If you're confused about how
to proceed in waking life, the hallways will most likely
twist and turn, disorienting you as you try to find
your way. Try to acknowledge what in your waking
life needs to be decided, and have patience as you

untangle your mental corridors and find the best course of action.

What Freud Would Say:	In *The Interpretation of Dreams*, Freud argued that rooms with open doorways represent a woman's vagina, and regarding the visual symbolism of staircases, he said, "Steps, ladders, or staircases, or, as the case may be, walking up or down them, are representations of the sexual act."
What Jung Would Say:	The house is a metaphor for the Self—Jung famously referred to the house as the "mansion of the soul." Through dreaming, you will learn about aspects of the Self that you have previously repressed or obscured.
Cultural Context:	Just how complex is your dream hallway? Semantically speaking, a maze and a labyrinth are two different structures. A maze is intended to confuse, with branching passages and dead ends. A classical labyrinth has only one path to the center, and while elaborate, is not difficult to navigate. In Greek mythology, Crete's King Minos commissioned an enormous labyrinth to hold the Minotaur, a half-man, half-bull creature born when the king's wife mated with a beautiful white bull. The Athenian Theseus sought to kill the Minotaur, and did so with help from the king's daughter, Ariadne. Ariadne gave Theseus a thread to carry through the labyrinth that would help him

retrace his steps. When he arrived at the center, he slew the Minotaur with a magical sword.

Related Images: Attic (p. 24); Basement (p. 26); Home, Childhood (p. 136); Kitchen (p. 151); Rooms, Secret (p. 199); Rooms, Unused (p. 202)

24.   **CRIME, COMMITTING**

Common
Manifestations: In this dream, you're the criminal. You watch yourself doing something you'd never attempt in real life—maybe you steal a computer from your company or slip some retail merchandise into your coat without paying for it. Some versions are more violent—you attack someone you know, beat someone senseless, even take another person's life. Perhaps after you commit the murder, you are consumed with the need to dispose of the dead body, but encounter one obstacle after another—the hole you dig isn't deep enough, or the hiding place you choose is more conspicuous than you first thought. As you experience these dreams, you may be deeply troubled by your actions or feel no remorse at all.

Variations: A similar dream focuses not on committing the crime, but on being captured, punished, and perhaps executed for it.

Occurrence: The dream of burying a dead body arises often during
                 adolescence and early adulthood.

The Spin: Imagining yourself as a criminal might allude to a
                 need for control; if you feel dominated or threatened
                 in your waking life, this dream scenario could be
                 viewed as a way to regain power. If you've attacked
                 someone you know, perhaps you're trying to forestall
                 an unpleasant event. Does that person harbor embar-
                 rassing information about you? Are you worried your
                 position at work or in a relationship will be usurped?
                 Often, dreaming that you've robbed someone else
                 points to unconscious feelings of envy, of wanting
                 something or some characteristic that the other
                 person has.

???   Interestingly, the vision of burying a dead body
                 points to your own struggles with identity—the per-
                 son you attack may actually be a particular aspect of
                 your own psyche. In order to achieve acceptance—
                 social, familial, or spousal—you may feel the need to
                 "kill off" or submerge the parts of your personality
                 deemed undesirable. (This could also be a sign that
                 you are trying to be someone you're not, or perhaps
                 you're not being true to yourself.) If, in the dream,
                 you feel no remorse for the crime you commit, you
                 were probably relieved to excise the parts of your per-
                 sonality that were holding you back. The fear of being
                 "caught" may indicate that you worry someone will
                 discover the unsavory traits you've been trying to

hide. Dreams that focus on capture and punishment are usually an expression of guilt—either for actions you have taken in waking life, or for negative/self-destructive feelings you have harbored.

What Freud
Would Say:

In *The Interpretation of Dreams*, Freud related the story of a friend who dreamt he was standing outside his home with a woman when the police arrived and arrested him for infanticide. Freud discovered that the man had been conducting a secret affair with a married woman. The two had practiced the withdrawal method of birth control, and the dream occurred directly after one of their interludes. Freud concluded that the dream arrest for infanticide was a form of wish fulfillment, because the man had been worried that this method of preventing pregnancy would be ineffective. In Freud's words, "It gave you reassurance that you had not procreated a child, or, what amounts to the same thing, that you had killed a child."

What Jung
Would Say:

The "you" who commits the crime might represent your Shadow archetype—the dark part of your personality that also serves as a creative wellspring. For Jung, no true spiritual or psychological growth could take place without acknowledgment of and reconciliation with the Shadow.

Cultural
Context:

Dreams of committing a crime open a window on the ways in which the mind makes decisions about morality.

Fixating on the fear of getting caught or punished indicates a basic instinct toward self-preservation. These types of reflexive decisions are addressed in the work of psychologist Lawrence Kohlberg, who identified a hierarchy of decision making called the Stages of Moral Development. He studied eighty-four boys over twenty years, posing a series of moral dilemmas and charting their responses over time. The six stages are as follows:

- **Stage One (begins in ages 3 to 5):** Making decisions based on punishment or magnitude of the act. (I don't shove sandwiches in the DVD player because I don't want to get caught.)

- **Stage Two (begins in ages 6 to 8):** Making decisions based on self-interest. (I took a cookie from my best friend because I was hungry.)

- **Stage Three:** Making decisions based on pleasing other people or maintaining the status quo. (I didn't drive faster than the legal speed limit because it would make my mother upset.)

- **Stage Four:** Making decisions because of respect for a higher authority; the law must be obeyed. (I don't speed because it is against the law.)

- **Stage Five:** Making decisions that prioritize the will of the majority and the welfare of society, while recognizing that sometimes human needs and laws conflict. (I drive the speed limit, even though I might lose my job if I'm late for work.)

- **Stage Six:** Making decisions based on your own internalized standards of right or wrong, regardless of opinions or legal restrictions. (I drive the speed limit because it's the right thing to do.)

Related Images: Crime, Victim of (p. 70); Death of Loved One (Unrelated to Actual Death) (p. 73); Death, Your Own (p. 76)

25. 📷   **CRIME, VICTIM OF**

Common Manifestations: You are the victim of a crime. Perhaps you catch someone breaking into your house or stealing your car. Or a menacing stranger attacks you, intent on sexual assault. The common thread in this dream is a feeling of powerlessness and panic. No matter what you try, you are unable to deter the perpetrator from his task. You hide, but he finds you. You run, but he runs faster. You fight, but he overpowers you. Ultimately, you cannot prevent the crime, nor the damage you suffer because of it.

Variations: The same feelings of helplessness arise when you dream of witnessing a violent attack or crime, yet can do nothing to stop it. To take this theme to an extreme, someone in your dream might actually kill you (p. 76).

The Spin:

For people who have been victimized in waking life, this dream has obvious posttraumatic implications. Some psychoanalysts believe that reliving these experiences in your dream state can be more therapeutic than tormenting. Under close supervision, and with the help of guided imagery and lucid dream techniques, the victim has the chance to "rewrite the script," and in doing so, to regain a measure of agency and power. But experts unanimously caution that if someone dreams of being abused with no waking-life memory of the experience, one can never simply assume that the dream represents a buried or repressed real-life memory.

If you have no such history of victimization, this dream might point to you feeling bulldozed, or taken advantage of, in waking life. Does an authority figure delight in lording power over you? Have you been on the losing end of an important battle of wills in a job, relationship, or family bond? Dreaming of sexual assault in particular can dramatize feelings of humiliation or submission. Helplessly witnessing an act of violence against someone else may reinforce feelings of impotence in the real world.

If Recurrent:

Perhaps the power struggle is a conflict taking place within your own psyche. You could be hamstrung by guilt, bullied by your own superego. Freud considered the superego to be the conscience of the personality—think of it as a politically correct internal policeman.

What Freud
Would Say:

In one of Freud's classic reversals, he claimed that when someone (particularly a woman) dreamed of being attacked or victimized, it actually represented the dreamer's unconscious wish to submit sexually to the attacker. Freud believed that the mind arranged to depict the assignation as forced so that the dreamer didn't have to accept responsibility for having the wish. He also claimed that dreams of burglars or thieves pointed to "infantile reminiscence," because dark figures hovering in the bedroom often turned out to be parents checking on their children and waking them from nightmares.

What Jung
Would Say:

Authors and dream experts Maeve Ennis and Jennifer Parker use this dream to make an interesting connection to Jung, invoking his theory of compensation. This theory states that the dream sphere allows free rein to thoughts and feelings that are difficult to express in the real world. Thus, someone who has problems expressing aggression in waking life will "compensate" for that problem by having vivid dreams that involve frequent or uncommon violence.

Cultural
Context:

Being the target of a relentless, savage criminal sparks a singular kind of panic and fear—the kind of fear Hollywood loves to exploit in countless horror movies, from the slasher oeuvres of Freddy (*A Nightmare on Elm Street*), Jason (*Friday the 13th*), and Michael Myers (*Halloween*) to more highly regarded suspense classics such as 1955's *The Night of the Hunter*. These movies get great mileage out of tense chase scenes where the villain always stays one step ahead of the victim—a superhuman prescience that recalls the peculiar illogic of the dream world. In *The Night of the Hunter*, Robert Mitchum portrays a disturbed ex-con, the "Reverend" Harry Powell, who stalks two young children after marrying and then killing their mother, hoping the kids will reveal the whereabouts of a secret stash of cash. In his "Great Movies" essay on the film, Roger Ebert describes a pivotal chase scene: "Soon the children are fleeing down the dream-river in a small boat, while the Preacher follows them implacably on the shore; this beautifully stylized sequence uses the logic of nightmares, in which no matter how fast one runs, the slow step of the pursuer keeps the pace."

Related Images: Chased, Being (p. 48); Death, Your Own (p. 76); Paralysis/Running in Slow Motion (p. 178)

26. 📷 ## DEATH OF LOVED ONE (UNRELATED TO ACTUAL DEATH)

Common Manifestations: In this especially traumatic dream, you are faced with the death of someone you care deeply about. Perhaps in the dream you witnessed the illness, accident, or sudden death without any power to change the outcome. Or maybe you heard about the death secondhand, or entered the dream already at the funeral. Your dream reaction to the death, likewise, could run the gamut from overpowering shock and grief to surprisingly blasé acceptance.

This dream involves the death of a person who is still alive in your waking life. For more on dream visits from an already deceased friend or loved one, see p. 79.

Occurrence: These dreams often arise in periods of great life change—getting married, starting a family, sending your kids off to college, and even retiring.

The Spin: Modern dream experts believe that, in the same way sex dreams aren't really about having sex, dreaming of someone's death seldom predicts an actual death or reveals a secret wish for that person to die. Dreams of death are primarily signifiers of transformation and transition—of turning over a new leaf or moving on to a new phase of your life. If the person who dies in the dream is your significant other, it can signal the existence of an emotional distance in the relationship that troubles you. Or, in your dream you could be mourning the end of the relationship itself. The dead character in your dream might even symbolize a facet of your own personality that has been neglected or repressed. As with other dreams that rely heavily on symbolism, paying attention to the nature of the dream death (and to your reactions within the dream setting) can provide an opportunity to find parallels with difficult real-life situations.

What Freud Would Say:

Freud considered this dream a classic case of wish fulfillment; he believed strongly that the dreamer wished the person to die in real life—a wish that may have originated in early childhood or with more recent events. The grief one feels in the dream over the death is the dream censor's way of processing the guilt that comes from having the wish in the first place. More recently, some Freudian analysts have modified that theory to state that such a dream hints at waking-life feelings of hostility toward the person who dies, and that the dream provides a safe, acceptable forum for airing those resentments.

What Jung Would Say:

Jung believed that dreams of death seldom were meant literally. In fact, in a lecture entitled "The Practical Use of Dream-Analysis," he said, "When it really is a question of death, dreams speak another language." For Jung, dream-death symbolized profound life change, or a significant change in one's thought/behavior patterns. Also, the nature of the death in the dream indicates how difficult or painful the process of change is for the dreamer. If the gender of the dead person is somehow significant, it may be that your unconscious masculine (Animus) or feminine (Anima) energies need attention.

Related Images: Death, Your Own (p. 76); Deceased Loved One, Visit from (p. 79)

---

27.   **DEATH, YOUR OWN**

Common
Manifestations:

You're dreaming of your own death. It could be death from a disease, an accident, or a violent crime. Sometimes the sensation is quite immediate—you can feel your life slipping away. But occasionally you participate in the dream scene as a kind of omniscient observer; you can see your own behavior as well as the responses that other characters in the dream have to you and your death.

Variations:

This category also encompasses suicide dreams.

The Spin:

In many cases, dreaming of your death expresses a wish to avoid responsibility for a difficult situation in your waking life; after all, death is the ultimate escape from a problem. If the dream is a suicide, you may be feeling trapped in a problem, with no foreseeable way out except to "end it all." (This doesn't necessarily imply that you have contemplated suicide, merely that your dreaming mind wants your problem to go away quickly and permanently.) If you are killed in the dream, try to describe your executioner. Is it someone you know? What characteristics does this person have? Do any of the characteristics correspond to a person or a situation in your waking life? If you can identify what it is you're running from, it might help you confront the problem directly and brainstorm a more productive solution.

Death (and birth, for that matter) also serve as common dream metaphors for big life changes—recent endings or new beginnings. Perhaps you have been recently widowed, or are struggling with empty-nest syndrome, or have recently lost a job or started a new career. You may unknowingly view the rite of passage as the "death" of a certain part of your life or personality. It's common to take some time to adapt to a new situation, and mulling over the attendant grief and conflicting emotions in the dream scenario may help you cope.

If Recurrent: 	If you have these dreams often, take them seriously. It may be a symptom of depression, a sign that you're on the wrong path, or a warning that you need to extricate yourself from a painful or self-destructive situation in your waking life.
What Freud Would Say:	As he hypothesized with dreams of sex, Freud believed that people did not remember dreaming of their own deaths because the concept would be too traumatic to the conscious mind. So what he called the internal dream censor chose more benign imagery to illustrate

the death motif. For example, Freud believed that a dream of missing a train (p. 61) really alluded to missing an "appointment" with death.

What Jung Would Say:

Dreams of your own death send a message that, for the sake of your own inner growth, it's time to move forward and leave behind certain aspects of your old self—negative attitudes, unhealthy habits, or unproductive emotions such as guilt and bitterness. In doing so, you open yourself up to greater enlightenment and self-acceptance. In this way, Jungian dream analyst Jeremy Taylor actually considers dreams of murder and suicide to be metaphorically positive, because they imply the willingness to exert conscious effort to walk away from who you used to be and to reinvent yourself. (Of course, he insists that these thoughts should not be processed literally—he clearly means the figurative death of your old self, not a literal ending of life.)

Cultural Context:

Two popular old wives' tales revolve around the presence of death in your dreams. First is the notion that if you dream of falling (p. 107) and actually hit the ground, you will die and never wake up. The second is simpler: If you die in a dream, it means you will die before you wake. Both are patently false.

Related Images:

Crime, Victim of (p. 70); Death of Loved One (Unrelated to Actual Death) (p. 73); Deceased Loved One, Visit from (p. 79)

28.   **DECEASED LOVED ONE, VISIT FROM**

Common
Manifestations:

In this dream, a person close to you visits from beyond the grave. The feelings this apparition evokes could range from bittersweet happiness at the reunion to debilitating sadness when loss overwhelms you. You might be able to converse with your dream vision about subjects mundane and profound. Or the transmission may only go one way: The person in your dream delivers a message to you without hearing anything you have to say in return.

Occurrence:

These dreams often arise in periods of great life change—getting married, starting a family, sending your kids off to college, and even retirement.

The Spin:

It's tempting to believe that this dream is truly a clairvoyant message from the spirit realm. Indeed, only you can vouch for the authenticity of your vision. Often, however, the dead character in your dream may symbolize a facet of your own personality that has been neglected or repressed and is only now coming to light. Your unconscious mind chose that particular person to deliver its message. Dreams of death are primarily signifiers of transformation and transition—of turning over a new leaf or moving on to a new phase of your life.

What Freud Would Say:	Freud considered these and other types of death dreams classic cases of wish fulfillment; he believed strongly that the dreamer wished the person to die in real life—a wish that may have originated in early childhood or with more recent events. The grief one feels in the dream over the death is the dream censor's way of processing the guilt that comes from having the wish in the first place. More recently, some Freudian analysts have modified that theory to state that such a dream hints at waking-life feelings of hostility toward the person who dies, and that the dream provides a safe, acceptable forum for airing those resentments.
What Jung Would Say:	Jung, too, believed that dreams of death seldom were meant literally. In fact, in a lecture entitled "The Practical Use of Dream-Analysis," he said, "When it really is a question of death, dreams speak another language." For Jung, dream-death symbolized profound life change, or a significant change in one's thought/behavior patterns. If the gender of the dead person is somehow significant, it may be that your unconscious masculine (Animus) or feminine (Anima) energies need attending to.
Cultural Context:	One of the most famous spirit visions in literature is the visitation upon Hamlet of his father's ghost. Hamlet's father reveals that he was murdered by his own brother, Claudius, who poured poison in his ear as he

slept. Claudius then became king and married Hamlet's mother, Gertrude. The ghost father urges Hamlet to exact revenge for his death. One of the many beauties of this play is the sheer ambiguity of Hamlet's vision; although the ghost's revelations set the plot in motion, Hamlet is never really sure if the vision is authentic or not—one of the many causes of his debilitating indecision. And if one applies here the notion that visions of deceased people represent aspects of the dreamer's own personality, then clearly Hamlet's father's ghost is the passionate embodiment of Hamlet's own feelings of betrayal and jealousy toward his duplicitous mother.

Related Images: Angels (p. 16); Death of Loved One (Unrelated to Actual Death) (p. 73); Death, Your Own (p. 76)

29.   **DESERT ISLAND**

Common Manifestations: You are stranded on a desert island. This could be a cause for celebration—lots of sun, sand, and quiet, and all the fresh fish, coconuts, and mangos you can eat. No boss to get on your back or rush-hour traffic to fight. What's not to like?

Variations: Desert island dreams could also have the qualities of a nightmare, a dream of deprivation in which you are unable to find adequate food and water, fear attack from wild animals or sharks, and yearn for rescue.

Occurrence:
This dream often arises at times of great emotional stress, or during profound life changes that engender anxiety or grief (pregnancy, death, divorce, job loss).

The Spin:
☺

These dreams are primarily about isolation, whether that isolation is desired or feared. It could be that you long to get away from it all, to leave your responsibilities and everyday stresses behind. For dream dictionary author Sandra Thomson, the image of a desert island reveals a need to find a safe place (internal or external) to recharge your emotional batteries and renew your zest for life, especially if the island in your dream features lush foliage and waterfalls. If you recognize the island in your dream, you may be harkening back to an easier, idyllic time in your life. It's possible that taking a "mental vacation" in your dream will bring you the relaxation you seek, but consider the dream a gentle, unconscious request to assess your life and remove needless, excessive stress.

☹ ♡ ???

Ominous desert-island dreams, on the other hand, speak to isolation's dark side—estrangement from loved ones, loneliness, alienation. One man's Shangri-la is another man's Alcatraz. And if you never learned to swim or you suffer from hydrophobia (fear of water), what could be more terrifying than being stranded on an island, with no tools or skills to facilitate your escape? If you fear abandonment, this dream may reflect waking-life feelings of emotional exile. Try to reconnect with those around you;

you will often find that others share the worries and fears that you harbor, and that you're not as alone as you thought.

What Freud Would Say:

Freud does not address dreams of desert islands per se. In *The Interpretation of Dreams*, he argued that water images evoked memories of the womb and birth, and regressive thoughts of childhood. Dreams in which the water, in whatever form, turned sinister could indicate anxiety about sex and repression of forbidden thoughts of bed-wetting.

What Jung Would Say:

For Jung, water was often representative of feminine energy (the Anima) and the sea was the symbol of the collective unconscious, "because unfathomed depths lie concealed beneath its reflecting surface." Feelings of emotional isolation—of being weighed down by "secret" or shameful thoughts—often prompt dreams of abandonment on a "lonely island." Jung termed it this way: "Isolation by a secret . . . causes an activation of the unconscious and produces something similar to the illusions and hallucinations that beset lonely wanderers in the desert, seafarers, and saints."

Cultural Context:

One of life's great ironies is that feelings of isolation are universal; you might feel as if no one understands what you're going through, but the person next to you feels the very same way. Poet and clergyman John Donne underscores mankind's inexorable interconnection in his 1624 "Meditation XVII," a sermon that includes the famous verse: "No man is an island entire of itself; every man is a piece of the continent, a part of the main. If a clod be washed away by the sea, Europe is the less, as well as if a promontory were, as well as if a manor of thy friend's or of thine own were; any man's death diminishes me, because I am involved in mankind. And therefore never send to know for whom the bell tolls; it tolls for thee."

Related Images: Beach/Ocean (p. 28); Drowning/Breathing Underwater (p. 84); Lost, Being (p. 155); Water (p. 230)

---

30. 📷   **DROWNING/BREATHING UNDERWATER**

Common Manifestations: You are somehow trapped underwater—perhaps you are inside a structure filled with water that prevents you from catching any air, or you may be too deep to reasonably consider reaching the surface. The feeling of holding your breath, of running out of air, makes your heart beat faster. You may also be struggling to keep your head above water, but rough seas repeatedly drag you under. You struggle and panic, knowing your life is in danger.

Variations: A surprising variation on this dream is that, after flailing around in fear of drowning, you finally give up and resign yourself to death. At the moment you open your mouth to suck in a lungful of water, you discover, to your shock and delight, that you are breathing normally and the water does not harm you at all. You are breathing as easily and naturally underwater as you would on dry land. This is a rare instance in which a nightmare turns out happily in the end.

Occurrence:

This dream might first arise during adolescence—when hormones keep your emotions revved high and you first begin to test your problem-solving skills—and then recur intermittently throughout your adult life.

The Spin:
???

Though images of floating or swimming can be very peaceful (p. 230), this dream has more ominous undertones. Traditionally, water has symbolized deep feelings as well as the unknown ("still waters run deep"). The sensation of struggling against—and being defeated by—something so vast and powerful is an apt metaphor for how overwhelmed you can feel by your emotions, or by a seemingly intractable situation. Perhaps you are stuck in a stressful rut right now and don't see any way out.

So here's the up side. At the moment you realized you were going to drown, you stopped fighting. According to Gillian Holloway, author of *The Complete Dream Book*, by opening your mouth and breathing underwater, you drew upon an inner resourcefulness and strength you didn't know you had. This is your mind's way of saying you have the tools inside to deal

with whatever life throws at you. You just need to
know when to open your mouth and make that leap
of faith.

What Freud Would Say:	Water images evoke memories of the womb and birth, and regressive thoughts of childhood. Dreams in which the water turns sinister could indicate anxiety about sex and repression of forbidden thoughts of bed-wetting.
What Jung Would Say:	Water is often representative of feminine energy (the Anima) and symbolizes the mystery of the unconscious. Drowning implies an intimidation or reluctance about exploring the psyche, but the image of breathing underwater indicates that your efforts will bear fruit.
Cultural Context:	As formidable dream metaphors go, it's hard to surpass the vast, unforgiving ocean—its size, depth, and power dwarf the individual. The specter of drowning sparks a fear that relates as much to feeling powerless and insignificant as it does to the fear of death. Forget the danger posed by scaling the Himalayas—scientists have long held that the deep ocean is the most extreme environment on Earth.

The deepest part of the ocean, roughly two hundred miles (320 km) southwest of Guam, is the
Challenger Deep of the Marianas Trench, at 35,802
feet (10,912 m) deep. That's about six thousand feet
(1,830 m) deeper than Mount Everest is tall. At that

depth, the seascape is as foreign as a visit to Mars: No light penetrates the water, and marine life consists mostly of bleached-out phosphorescent fish (with no eyes—they're not necessary) and the occasional colony of red algae. The hydrostatic pressure (the weight of the water on top of you) in the Marianas Trench is more than eight tons per square inch (1.1 metric tons per sq cm)—the equivalent of fifty jumbo jets pressing down on one person. Only two people, Jacques Piccard and Don Walsh, have made it to the floor of the Marianas Trench, and they did it together, in 1960, in a specially equipped bathyscaphe able to withstand the crushing pressure. No one has attempted it since.

As for scuba diving—the only way in which humans are currently able to breathe underwater—it's commonly accepted that dives deeper than two hundred feet (60 m) seriously affect a diver's ability to perform the simplest mental or motor tasks and can cause brain damage. Currently, the deepest recorded human scuba dive is 1,044 feet (318.25 m), set by Nuno Gomes in the Red Sea in June 2005.

Related Images: Beach/Ocean (p. 28); Flying (p. 124); Water (p. 230)

31. 📷   **EARS**

Common
Manifestations: You might dream that you or someone close to you suddenly sprouts oversized or highly prominent ears.

This might be accompanied by the surprising ability to hear the tiniest sounds; you are hyperattuned to all ambient noise, and you might even be able to eavesdrop on private conversations from a long way away.

Variations: The flip side of the bionic-hearing dream is to dream of being deaf—you see someone's lips moving, but all is silent, and no sounds reach your ears. Or perhaps you are overwhelmed by a specific noise—a jet engine, the roar of a crowd—and you can't hear someone nearby who tries to communicate with you. An extreme version of this dream is to picture yourself with no ears at all.

The Spin: Dreams of an oversized pair of ears may be a message
???   urging you to open yourself to outside information and to stay tapped in to the political and interpersonal undercurrents swirling around you ("I'm all ears" or "keeping an ear to the ground"). Or maybe you need to pay closer attention to the things people are telling you.

Dreams that involve the body or its specific parts are often coded holistic messages about the inner life of the dreamer. Losing a body part can signify a specific area of loss or pain in your life. Often, upon reflection, you realize you have failed to nurture an important part of yourself in order to fit in or to achieve a larger goal. If you dream of being deaf, perhaps there is a reality that you are unwilling to face ("to turn a deaf ear"). Or you are ignoring something that's obvious and right in front of your nose.

If Recurrent: Take such dreams seriously. Dreams that underscore the disconnect between what matters to you and how you conduct your life are intended as gentle warnings. Such compromises and inner censoring, when taken to extremes, are not natural or healthy for the psyche.

What Freud Would Say: According to dream dictionary author Sandra Thomson, Freud believed "our superego/conscience was mostly auditory," and she makes the point that perhaps dreaming of deafness unconsciously underscores the need to ignore internal censoring or judgments. As for the source of the things we hear while dreaming, Freud famously said in *The Interpretation of Dreams*, "Dreams are the guardians of sleep, and not its disturbers." He believed that external sensory stimuli, especially ambient sounds, were regularly incorporated into the dream scenario as a way for the body to maintain the sleep state. Thus, you may dream of hearing cannons during a real-life thunderstorm, or of a nagging telephone ringing when your alarm clock goes off. Freud went so far as to argue that all speech in dreams is "unoriginal"—meaning, it derives wholly from snippets of waking-life thoughts and conversations, cut up and reassembled to fit the particular dream-logic.

What Jung Would Say:	Though Jung did not address ear imagery directly, in his book *Dreams* he claimed that hearing a voice in one's dream "expresses some truth or condition that is beyond all doubt."

Physical Manifestation:	Although in your dream, you may experience deafness as a world of total silence, in the waking world such a reality is, for the most part, scientifically inaccurate. Anecdotal evidence suggests that some deaf people—who have been deaf since birth—perceive myriad sounds in their minds (a type of "inner voice") and, astonishingly, even dream with full soundtracks. In the absence of sensory input, the brain nevertheless is able to produce noise and approximate "speech," though such speech might not remotely correspond to a spoken language. Medical researchers have found that schizophrenics who are deaf can suffer from auditory hallucinations, in the same way that blind schizophrenics are capable of visual hallucinations.

Related Images:	Eyes (p. 103); Mouth and Teeth (p. 166)

ELEVATORS, STAIRS, AND LADDERS

Common Manifestations:	Elevator dreams can carry positive or negative associations. You could be traveling by elevator to an important business appointment. Or, like Charlie in *Charlie and the Chocolate Factory*, your elevator ride could morph

into a magical flight up and across the sky. On the down side, you could be trapped in a stalled elevator as you feel claustrophobia kick in. Or the elevator loses power and freefalls with you in it, and the terror you feel at being trapped catapults you into wakefulness.

Dreams involving stairs or ladders, on the other hand, often involve a measure of physical effort. Perhaps you're running up or down the stairs to escape someone or something dangerous. Or you might be rushing to meet a person who is important to you. It might be a dream of frustration, where you climb and climb and yet finish in the same place you started (not unlike the staircases depicted in the M. C. Escher drawings *Relativity* and *Ascending and Descending*). Or you may be ascending a ladder or stairway up and up, into the ether (a stairway to heaven?).

Occurrence: This dream imagery may crop up when you're grappling with a particularly difficult decision or problem in your waking life.

The Spin: It may sound obvious, but elevator dream imagery
??? connotes movement. According to Sandra Thomson, author of *Cloud Nine: A Dreamer's Dictionary*, an elevator traveling between floors in your dream can represent the flow of thoughts from the unconscious to the conscious mind, or vice versa. But the implications may well be more concrete. Elevators that don't take you where you want to go speak to a tension

between what you want and where you are. Riding in an elevator that soars above its shaft is a lovely metaphor for biting off more than you can chew, whether at work or in a close relationship. On the flip side, a plummeting elevator mirrors the kind of topsy-turvy feeling you get when a particular aspect of your life spins out of control. Trying to connect the emotions you experience in the elevator to a situation in your waking life could bring insight to a challenge you're currently facing.

Stairs and ladders, on the other hand, often involve more tangible progress—striving for a specific goal, or attempting to effect change in your life. Conversely, climbing up or down a ladder to escape a fire, storm, or dangerous situation could indicate that you are avoiding a volatile life challenge or powerful emotions that threaten to overwhelm you.

What Freud Would Say:

Although Freud did not write of elevator imagery specifically, he did believe that his research showed staircase dreams—dreaming of walking or running up and down a set of stairs—to be thinly veiled metaphors for sexual intercourse. "We were soon in a position to show that staircases (and analogous things) were unquestionably symbols of copulation," he wrote in *The Interpretation of Dreams*. "It is not hard to discover the basis of the comparison: We come to the top in a series of rhythmical movements and with increasing breathlessness and then, with a few rapid leaps, we can get to the bottom again. Thus the rhythmical pattern of copulation is reproduced in going upstairs."

What Jung Would Say:	Elevators, stairs, and ladders are visual manifestations of the individuation process—the pursuit of a higher level of consciousness. (Conversely, climbing down a ladder or staircase into a pit or dark hole could point to a willingness to explore the mysteries of the unconscious.) Climbing a ladder or staircase often represents progress, whether physical or psychological. Such imagery also carries profound spiritual and historical implications. Jung believed that, to underscore the quest for spiritual knowledge, the collective unconscious invokes such mythological symbols as Jacob's Ladder (see "Cultural Context," below) and the Stairway of the Seven Planets—both allegorical elevators that facilitate the journey to a heavenly realm. Regarding the latter, he said, "The ascent was often represented by a ladder; hence the burial gift in Egypt of a small ladder for the *ka* of the dead. [*Ka* is a person's animating or life force.] The idea of an ascent through the seven spheres of the planets symbolizes the return of the soul to the sun-god from whom it originated, as we know for instance from [the works of fourth-century Latin astrologer] Firmicus Maternus."
Cultural Context:	The dream notion of using a ladder, stairway, or elevator to ascend into spiritual enlightenment harkens back to the story of Jacob's Ladder in the Old

Testament book of Genesis. After fleeing a family imbroglio, Jacob, wandering in the wilderness, lies down to rest and has a dream vision of God. In Jacob's dream, a great ladder begins on Earth and stretches into the sky, all the way to heaven. Angels were ascending and descending the ladder, and God presided at the top of the ladder. According to Jacob, "the Lord stood above it, and said, I am the Lord . . . I am with thee, and will keep thee in all places whither thou goest, and will bring thee again into this land. . . ." The story speaks strongly to humanity's need for spiritual communion, regardless of one's religious affiliation (in Jacob's vision, the angels relay messages back and forth to heaven), and the common perception of life as a journey, with some form of eternal life in the hereafter as a final destination.

Related Images: Angels (p. 16); Falling (p. 107); Mechanical Malfunction (p. 158); Paralysis/Running in Slow Motion (p. 178)

33.   **ELIMINATION, INAPPROPRIATE OR INCONVENIENT**

Common
Manifestations: On your travels about town, you are seized with an urgent need to use the bathroom. But you can't find a public toilet. Or you finally locate a toilet after much frantic searching, only to discover that the stalls are

occupied, soiled, or broken. Perhaps you locate a toilet, but it's out in the open, with no privacy at all. In some cases, you have already started using the toilet when you realize you're in full view of everyone. But no one seems to notice or care that you're taking care of embarrassing business in public.

Variations: A toilet is overflowing with waste, and you are unable to fix it.

Occurrence: The urgent-need-to-go dreams arise often in children, especially chronic bed-wetters, but it's a common theme for adults as well.

The Spin: Although these dreams, especially in children, may reflect a real physical need during the sleep phase (dreaming about using the bathroom instead of waking up to do so), in many cases the inability to find somewhere to relieve yourself is a statement of frustration. You may have so many real-world responsibilities that you have no time to address your own needs. Because excretion is associated with purging impurities from your system, you can look at this as a warning sign that you're building up negative or counterproductive energy that needs an outlet in order for you to maintain a healthy outlook. Similarly, the image of an overflowing toilet may point to habitually putting someone else's needs before your own—being the person that everyone else "dumps" on, if you will. As a result, you're stuck dealing with a lot of crap you didn't create but don't know what to do with.

If the salient feature of your dream is the embarrassment of having to urinate or defecate in public, then you may simply be struggling with feelings of shame or embarrassment at the thought of putting an aspect of your private life on public display. The fact that, in the dream, bystanders don't seem to know or care what you are doing indicates that the insecurity is without cause and comes from within.

What Freud Would Say: In *The Interpretation of Dreams*, Freud made several observations about these types of dreams. He made the obvious point—as others did before him—that dreaming of urination often reflects a legitimate physiological urge: "The symbolism of dreams with a urinary stimulus is especially transparent and has been recognized from the earliest times. The view was already expressed by Hippocrates that dreams of fountains and springs indicate a disorder of the bladder." And yet Freud also asserted that dreams of urination have "undisguisedly erotic imagery" and can represent hidden sexual wishes. He felt that excrement and defecation (in short, anal imagery) symbolized money as well as feelings of pride, aggression, and shame.

What Jung Would Say: Jung was fascinated with alchemy—the medieval philosophy that sought to turn such base metals as lead into gold. Jungian dream analyst Jeremy Taylor argues that Jung approached psychoanalysis with the same zeal—that if you have the courage and curiosity to confront the "excrement" of your life, it's possible to transform this life experience into your "gold," which in this case would be an authentic state of self-love and spiritual awareness. In his autobiography, *Memories, Dreams, Reflections*, Jung relates a bizarre and vivid dream he had at age twelve: "I saw before me the cathedral, the blue sky. God sits on His golden throne, high above the world—and from under the throne an enormous turd falls upon the sparkling new roof, shatters it, and breaks the walls of the cathedral asunder. So that was it! I felt an enormous, an indescribable relief . . . I wept for happiness and gratitude." He felt that God had sent him that dream directly, as proof that it was possible to have a one-on-one connection with a higher power, and it was the primary reason he devoted his life to the study of the human mind.

Cultural Context: Artemidorus, dream expert of ancient Greece, actually believed that dreams of defecation foretold carefree times and good luck for the dreamer. The ancient Romans had no qualms about public elimination; indeed, most citizens paid to use centrally located public toilets, which featured an ambitious system of freshwater sewage drains that ran underneath the buildings to carry away waste. Some public toilets seated as many as a hundred people at once, and the buildings served as informal meeting places, where men would socialize and conduct business while they went about their personal rituals. Indoor plumbing did not become a common feature of Western households until the middle of the nineteenth century, once the link was established between poor sanitary conditions and widespread disease outbreaks. Legend says a British plumber named Thomas Crapper developed the prototype for the flush toilet in 1872, but it's likely he was not the actual inventor.

Related Images: Communication Breakdown (p. 55); Nudity, Public (p. 175); Sex, Interrupted/Nowhere to Make Love (p. 206); Water (p. 230)

34.   **END OF THE WORLD**

Common Manifestations: You bear witness to the apocalypse. It might be a formidable natural disaster, a nuclear explosion, or a religious Judgment Day scenario. Death and destruction are all around, and the specter overwhelms you. Perhaps you merely observe the scene in horror, or you might be swept into the torment. Waking from the dream, you are at once terrified and relieved.

Occurrence: This dream might occur when you're facing traumatic life passages—divorce, death in the family, unemployment, or serious illness.

The Spin:	Although some might fear that such dreams are prophetic, it's more likely that the seismic shift is happening within, not without. Something Earth-shattering may have happened to you—a partner or family member has died, you've just been laid off from your job, a long-term relationship has ended—and it feels, metaphorically, like the end of the world. That's true, to a certain extent; after suffering a tragedy, your worldview is necessarily shaken and altered. But the silver lining, if one exists, is the dawn that follows the darkness. One phase ends, and a new one begins. Give yourself the time you need to process the raw emotions and adapt to your new situation. For more on dreams of natural disasters, see p. 172.
If Recurrent:	You may have tapped into your inner drama queen.
What Freud Would Say:	Freud, as an atheist, did not believe in any type of ultimate spiritual reckoning. But he did write that war was a fundamental expression of man's innate instinct toward hatred and aggression.
What Jung Would Say:	In Jung's autobiography, *Memories, Dreams, Reflections*, he related a disturbing hallucination he experienced in middle age. The vision was of a "frightful catastrophe," in which large tracts of continental Europe had flooded. Jung related how he "saw the mighty yellow waves, the floating rubble of civilization, and the drowned bodies of uncounted thousands. Then

For more on dreams of natural disasters, see p. 172.

the whole sea turned to blood." But shortly after this vision, Jung experienced the much more tender, healing dream of a "leaf-bearing" tree mysteriously covered with "sweet grapes full of healing juices" that he plucked and fed to the multitudes. The dream seems to have underscored Jung's deep Christian faith (given the strong death/rebirth imagery), and it served to solidify his commitment to the study of the human psyche as a way to illuminate the problems faced in twentieth-century life.

Cultural Context:

Written works throughout recorded history describe man's visions or prophecies about the end of the world—meaning, in this case, the ultimate religious-type apocalypse, not the inner-turmoil type. The most famous such works would be the Bible's New Testament book of Revelation, said to be written by John the Apostle, and the writings of the sixteenth-century physician and philosopher Nostradamus. Interestingly, some scholars believe that neither John the Apostle nor Nostradamus intended to prophesize future events in their writings, but rather wanted to chronicle and criticize important political and religious issues of their time, using cleverly coded language that allowed them to elude persecution. But it was exactly this extensive use of metaphor and cryptic language that allowed their work to be reinterpreted, over time, as literal prophecy.

Related Images: Death of Loved One (Unrelated to Actual Death)
(p. 73); Death, Your Own (p. 76); Natural Disasters:
Earthquakes, Hurricanes, Tornadoes, and Volcanoes
(p. 172)

35.   **EXAM/PUBLIC PERFORMANCE**

Common
Manifestations:
You are in a classroom to take a scheduled exam. But
when you look down at your test, you realize it's for a
completely different subject—one you have not studied
for, or know nothing about. The exam dream has infinite variations. You have overslept and are late for
your exam. Perhaps the test is written in another language, and you can't decipher a word of it. Or you
rush around in a dither, unable to find the room
where the test is taking place. Or you wake up on
the morning of the exam to realize that you have not
attended a single class all term, and yet must pass the
test in order to graduate.

Variations:
The fear of public performance dream has many kin-
dred elements to the exam dream: You're forced up on
stage to speak or perform, but you don't know your
lines; you're handed a musical instrument that you
don't know how to play; or you are expected to sing a
complicated aria, even though you couldn't carry a
tune with a bucket.

Occurrence: Though these dreams often evoke an academic setting, they usually manifest in postgraduation years, to people who are well established in a career.

The Spin: Being unprepared for a test is a classic anxiety dream and the rare dream image that can sometimes be interpreted literally. If you are preparing to take an important test, ask yourself if you are really prepared. If the answer is yes, but you still feel anxious, then this dream points to perfectionist tendencies—perhaps you lack the self-esteem to be truly confident, no matter how you excel. If an exam isn't on the horizon, could the dream be a metaphor for other tests you face, or for a sense of being scrutinized by someone else? Perhaps you recently received a promotion and are worried about whether you can succeed with the new responsibility. Introducing the specter of a public performance—with the implication that multitudes will hang on your every move—ratchets the pressure even higher.

 If the impending performance or test is unfair or illegible, try to identify the authority figure who's calling the shots. Is it someone you know? Does it represent someone in your life who is judging you or holding you to an impossible standard? Psychoanalyst Alexander Grinstein believes that dreaming of such "tests" indicates a fear of punishment or a fear of failure in sexual performance.

If Recurrent:	This might be a sign that your schedule is so over-loaded that you will never catch up with your many demands and responsibilities.
What Freud Would Say:	*The Interpretation of Dreams* addresses exam-anxiety dreams in surprising detail. Freud believed these dreams almost always recalled an actual test the dreamer had experienced in the past. But invariably, the test referenced in the dream was one the patient had passed quite easily. And so, because the anxiety prompted by the dream scenario had proven to be ill founded, Freud concluded that the dream anxiety probably "referred to the repetition of reprehensible sexual acts." And it goes without saying that performance anxiety has obvious Freudian connotations as well.
What Jung Would Say:	Failure dreams are symptoms of an anxious personality and recall fears of parental disapproval. The key to overcoming this perfectionism is to strive for greater self-acceptance.
Related Images:	Child, Forgetting or Misplacing (p. 51); The Impossible Task (p. 140)

36. **EYES**

Common Manifestations:	In your dream, you have sprouted an extra eye or two—in the center of your head or in the center of

your palms. Perhaps the eyes in your dream are hyper-bolically prominent—a giant eye looks down on you or multiple pairs of eyes follow your every move, even in your most private moments, rendering you something of a zoo specimen, à la Charlton Heston in *Planet of the Apes*.

Variations: One disturbing take on this dream is to imagine that something has blinded you—maybe a sharp object stabs you through the eye socket—or simply for some sudden and mysterious reason you are unable to see anything, or anyone, around you.

Occurrence: Such dreams might arise at a time when you are contemplating a large life change or actively pursuing a greater degree of self-awareness.

The Spin: Dreams that involve the body or its specific parts are
???   often coded holistic messages about the inner life of the dreamer. Historically and culturally, the eye has represented enlightenment and knowledge. Author Sandra Thomson notes the parallel between the English-language homophones *eye* and *I*, positing that the eye might symbolically represent the dreamer's ego, or self. Dreams of ultraprominent eyes may be a message urging greater vigilance, to be more aware of your emotional and political surroundings ("keep your eyes open"). Multiple eyes following your every move may also speak to feelings of conspicuousness—all

eyes are focused on you, or at least that's how you often feel.

Losing a body part can signify a specific area of loss or pain in your life. If you dream of blindness, have you lost sight of something important to you? Or maybe you have developed a "blind spot" in relation to an obvious problem or life stress and need to approach the issue from a fresh perspective.

If Recurrent: Take such dreams seriously. Dreams that underscore the disconnect between what matters to you and how you conduct your life are intended as gentle warnings. Pay closer attention to what fulfills you, and be forthright in grappling with any opportunities for psychic growth.

What Freud Would Say: Dreams with eye symbolism are usually disguised Oedipal wishes, or the desire for a man to have sex with his mother. Freud believed that the blinding of Oedipus at the end of the play *Oedipus Rex* (see "What Freud Would Say," p. 213) was a veiled symbol of castration.

What Jung Would Say: The archetype of the blind man usually symbolizes inner wisdom, but also, as in the Old Testament tale of Samson (see "Cultural Context," p. 131), can symbolize a punishment or sacrifice for transgressions.

Cultural Context: Almost every major culture and religion throughout recorded history has employed eye imagery to connote special knowledge or inner vision. In Egyptian mythology, Horus—son of Ra and god of the sky—was usually depicted as a falcon, his right eye representing the Sun and his left eye the Moon. In Norse mythology, the god Odin, seeker of wisdom, plucked out one of his own eyes in exchange for a drink from the magical well waters of Mimir, the primal Norse god of knowledge. In Renaissance art, an eye surrounded by the Sun's rays symbolized the watchful eye of a Christian God. In the Bible, blindness often corresponded to living in "spiritual darkness," before a person embraced conversion or religious teachings.

The "third eye" is a common metaphor for higher knowledge. In yogic philosophy, the third eye in the center of the forehead is the sixth of the seven chakras (or centers of spiritual energy) in the human body, responsible for intuition and imagination. In religious art of the Aztecs, Native Americans, Hindus, Muslims, and Hebrews, among others, the third eye is often depicted in the center of the palm—a mystical symbol that conveys the simultaneous impression of omniscience (the all-seeing eye) and omnipotence (the all-powerful hand). The Tibetan deity White Tara, the Divine Mother, is portrayed with seven eyes (three in her head, one in the palm of each hand, and one in the sole of each foot). When a hand with an eye is shown by itself, fingers pointed down, it's a *hamsa*, a talisman common to many Middle

Eastern and Mediterranean cultures, thought to protect the bearer from the "evil eye."

Related Images: Ears (p. 87); Mouth and Teeth (p. 166)

37.   **FALLING**

Common
Manifestations: You might be traversing a cliff face or just taking a stroll down the sidewalk. But when you start to fall, you realize that you have tumbled into an abyss. You feel powerless, with nothing to tether you. The falling sensation continues and grows stronger until you wake up, heart pounding.

Variations: You are walking, perhaps running, and you fall suddenly, hard. The force of your dream-fall jerks you awake.

Occurrence: This is probably the most commonly reported dream, one that nearly everyone has experienced at one time or another.

The Spin: This classic anxiety dream is wonderfully evocative of the fear of losing control. In fact, that sense of helplessness and terror is so powerful that, as you fall, it almost always wakes you up before you hit the ground. (The notion that if you fall and hit the ground in the dream, then you will die and never wake up, is complete hokum.) The height from which you fall may represent the high expectations that you or others have for you and your worry about living up to them. Try to pinpoint what in the dream precipitates your fall. Were you rushing for some reason? Was there an obstacle in your path? Your unconscious is pushing you to identify and confront your anxiety—if you can understand why you are stressed, overwhelmed, or scared, you're more likely to find a practical remedy.

What Freud
Would Say:

Falling dreams are anxiety-based. In *The Interpretation of Dreams*, Freud claimed that, for women, the imagery of falling almost always has a sexual connotation, either describing "a surrender to erotic temptation" or judging oneself as "a fallen woman."

What Jung
Would Say:

Dreams of falling could predict an imminent period of rebirth. You may also be worried about losing face or self-esteem.

Physical
Manifestations:

During a falling dream, most people are jolted awake by one of two things: the fear that grips your psyche from the falling sensation itself, or a sudden muscle spasm as you imagine hitting the ground. The latter phenomenon is called a myoclonic jerk. Although the exact cause of myoclonic spasms is not known, many psychologists believe that as a person descends into REM sleep, muscle paralysis kicks in, and the brain may interpret this sensation as a loss of control. This prompts a dream of falling, and the muscle jerk becomes a physical reaction to the dream content. (Interestingly, hiccups are considered myoclonic jerks of the diaphragm.) The fluttery sensation you feel during your dream free-fall (or while riding a particularly swoopy roller coaster), commonly referred to as butterflies in the stomach, is part of the body's "fight or flight" response to stress. Hormones, including adrenaline, flood your system, causing an increase in heart rate and shallow breathing. Some medical experts believe that what causes the butterflies sensation is the constriction of blood vessels that serve the internal organs.

Related Images: Exam/Public Performance (p. 101); Lost, Being (p. 155)

---

38. **FATHER**

Common Manifestations:
Your dad plays a starring role in this dream. Perhaps you are dreaming of a new encounter, in which you say things you've never had the chance to say to each other. Or you may be living out a scene, positive or negative, played in waking life hundreds of times before—you and your dad laughing at the same jokes, playing sports, working on a home-repair project together, or arguing bitterly when he disapproves of a choice you've made.

Variations: You might also dream of your father's death, though
he is still alive in real life (p. 73). Or, even more
disturbingly, you may dream you are having sex with
your father (p. 211).

The Spin: It's easy to claim that the family patriarch symbolizes
 tradition and authority—this is true, to a certain extent,
but rarely are family relationships so unilateral. Parents
are only human, after all, and they come with their
own emotional baggage to contend with. To decode
what your dream dad is trying to tell you, you need
to pay attention to the dream's setting, time, and
background characters. How old are you in the dream?
At that age, how did you feel about your dad—was he
King of the World, or Mr. Do No Right? Where did
the dream take place, and what associations do you
have with that setting? Your mind chose to take you
back to this particular period for a reason—most likely
to shed light on a situation or problem you're currently
facing. It could be that you're becoming a parent
yourself, and your unconscious is sifting through
your history for advice and guidance. Understanding
the connection between your dream past and your
waking present could highlight unhealthy behavior
patterns, and with time and insight, history will cease
to repeat itself.

Dreams of death are primarily signifiers of transformation and transition—of turning over a new leaf
or moving on to a new phase of your life. Adolescents

often dream of one or both of their parents dying as a metaphoric expression of their growing independence. Dreams of having sex with your father are unlikely to be a symptom of repressed childhood abuse. Instead, the connection your unconscious is making may be more complex and metaphorical. Your current partner might simply share a significant personality trait with your father, and in real life you find yourself responding to him or her with the same old behavior patterns.

What Freud Would Say:

One could argue that Freud's bread and butter, the central hypotheses of his psychoanalytic theory, were the Oedipus and Electra complexes—that men unconsciously want to kill their fathers and have sex with their mothers, and that women want to kill their mothers and have sex with their fathers, and that both men and women spend a great deal of psychic energy repressing that realization. Freud believed strongly that young boys and girls view their same-sex parent as a rival for the other parent's affection and that it's not a stretch to imagine an impulsive, id-governed child wishing for a parent's death. In speaking of fathers and sons in ancient history, Freud observed, "The more unrestricted was the rule of the father in the ancient family, the more must the son, as his destined successor, have found himself in the position of an enemy, and the more impatient must he have been to become ruler himself through his father's death."

What Jung
Would Say:

Among Jung's many archetypes of the collective unconscious is the Spiritual Father, representative of what Jung called the "masculine" principle of light, spirit, and higher consciousness (contrasted with the more fertile, earthbound quality of the Great Mother archetype). The Jungian archetype that embodies the Spiritual Father in human form is the Wise Old Man—often portrayed as a mentor, priest, healer, or town elder. This is the earthly source of law and order, much as a parent sets the rules and presides over the family. Jung called the dream father "the embodiment of the traditional spirit as expressed in religion or a general philosophy of life. . . . He imprisons the dreamer in the world of the conscious mind and its values."

Related Images:

Death of a Loved One (Unrelated to Actual Death) (p. 73); Deceased Loved One, Visit from (p. 79); Mother (p. 163); Sex with Someone You Know (Not Your Partner) (p. 211)

39.

FEET, LEGS, AND SHOES

Common
Manifestations:

You're having trouble walking. Perhaps your feet are suddenly too big—or too small—in proportion to your body. Maybe you have injured your leg, ankle, or foot, and you are walking with a limp. You could be trying on, or walking in, strange, new, or unfamiliar shoes. Or the dream may not be about your feet at all; perhaps you are tracking a set of footprints in the mud, snow, or sand, searching for someone you can't see in the distance.

Variations:
A more extreme dream is one in which you are paralyzed, unable to walk, or have lost a leg or foot through violence or amputation.

The Spin:
Dreams that involve specific parts of the body are often coded holistic messages about the inner life of the dreamer. The feet are symbolic of walking your life's path, of making progress and being independent in the waking world. If you're having trouble walking in the dream, ask yourself whether an obstacle or stress in your waking life has brought you to a metaphoric standstill. According to dream analyst Gillian Holloway, walking barefoot could hint at feelings of vulnerability, or a need to be "grounded." Conversely, shoes often represent a dreamer's identity; if you dream of wearing or trying on new, unusual, or uncomfortable shoes, your unconscious might be mulling over the assumption of a new identity: a career change, a recent breakup, impending parenthood. How do the shoes feel in your dream? Are they a good fit? Do they suit your style? Or is every step a painful effort, and the style bizarre and incongruous? Addressing such questions could tap in to your intuition as you contemplate a major life change. Dream dictionary author

Sandra Thomson notes the pun between the "sole" of the foot and the "soul," or a need to connect with your soul; the image of the heel can likewise allude to a yen for healing.

If the dream of losing a body part does not coincide with a similar development in your waking life, it can signify a specific episode of loss or pain. Often, upon reflection, you realize you have failed to nurture an important part of yourself in order to fit in or to achieve a larger goal. That you struggle against immobility in the dream indicates that at least part of you wants to continue moving forward. If you dream of losing a leg or foot—or even just your ability to walk—your unconscious might be telling you that an important relationship in your life, whether work, family, or life partner, is not supporting you enough to get you where you need to go. In a similar way, seeing footprints in a dream signifies absence—an opportunity wasted, or a person who isn't there for you in the way you expect. Footprints can also positively connote pride in your heritage—are you following in someone's footsteps?

If Recurrent: Take such dreams seriously—they underscore what matters to you and are intended as gentle warnings. Such compromises and inner censoring, when taken to extremes, are not natural or healthy for the psyche.

What Freud Would Say:	As with dreams of being chased (p. 48), Freud felt that dreaming of an inability to run indicated that the dreamer wanted to be caught. Not surprisingly, Freud believed this unconscious desire had a sexual connotation, for women especially; the dream represented a wish to be caught and ravished.
What Jung Would Say:	Jung believed that dreams provided a window into the mysteries of the psyche and afforded great opportunity for self-knowledge. For him, the characters in a dream usually represented aspects of one's own personality: "To go for a walk is to wander along paths that lead nowhere in particular; it is both a search and a succession of changes." So, an inability to walk would indicate an unwillingness to explore the psyche and to address the potential for life change.
Cultural Context:	The notion of feet as symbols of independence and, obliquely, of power, is illustrated throughout history by the attempts of people in power to control other people by controlling their mobility. In the United States, runaway slaves recaptured by their masters had their Achilles tendons severed—a punishment that preserved the ability to walk but prevented them from ever running again. An example with disturbing longevity is the Chinese practice of foot binding. Traced back to the seventh century BCE and formally outlawed by the Chinese government in 1911, binding was intended to slow or even halt the growth of a

woman's feet by wrapping them tightly at an early age, sometimes as early as five years old. A bound foot, considered aesthetically ideal and sexually desirable, could not realistically support the body of a full-grown woman. The practical consequence, therefore, was to limit a woman's mobility, keeping her housebound and thus ensuring her purity or chasteness. Perhaps unsurprisingly, foot binding was essentially restricted to the upper classes. In peasant communities women worked alongside the men; families could not afford to be saddled with helpless mothers and daughters.

Related Images: Fingers and Hands (p. 116); Paralysis/Running in Slow Motion (p. 178)

40. **FINGERS AND HANDS**

Common Manifestations: Dreams of your hands and fingers often manifest in images of highly prominent or distinctive appendages. Your hands may be disproportionately large compared to your body, or they may be conspicuously engaged: making something, gesticulating forcefully, or touching something or someone.

Variations: A disturbing version is to dream that your fingers and hands are incapacitated—perhaps they are tied up, handcuffed, or somehow injured. Taking this incapacity to the extreme is to dream of missing one or more of your fingers—or that one or both of your hands have been amputated.

Occurrence:

Negative or disturbing types of hand and finger dreams might arise at a time when you are feeling creatively blocked or helpless in your life—perhaps you're an artist having trouble with your latest work, you are recovering from a serious illness, or, as a senior citizen, you chafe against limited physical abilities.

The Spin:

Dreams that involve the body or its specific parts are often coded holistic messages about the inner life of the dreamer. The hands are a strong tactile metaphor for creativity, action, and independence. In waking life, are you "trying your hand" at something? Feeling tightfisted for some reason? Or asking someone for a helping hand? For dream analyst Gillian Holloway, hands represent the ability of a dreamer to grasp and control her destiny, and fingers represent individuality—think of the singular nature of a fingerprint. Both hands and fingers are important tools for body language and nonverbal communication: Crossing the hands over the body is a common sign of defensiveness and rejection, just as pointing a finger at someone else is often interpreted as rude or aggressive.

???

Dreaming of hands that are injured or nonfunctioning speaks to a power imbalance in your life. Handcuffs not only reinforce the straightforward message of losing or relinquishing control ("my hands are tied");

they carry overtones of sexual submission as well. Losing a body part can signify a specific area of loss or pain in your life. Because the hands are a crucial symbol of activity, dreams of having a hand cut off can represent feelings of powerlessness and impotence—especially when the dream focuses on all that you *can't* do for yourself. Some dream theorists go so far as to ascribe individual meanings to dreams about certain fingers on the hand (the ring finger symbolizes commitment, the index finger authority, and so on), and so the loss of or inability to use a particular finger can point to a crisis in a specific area of your life.

If Recurrent: Take such dreams seriously. Dreams that highlight feelings of frustration and powerlessness are often wake-up calls to take action in your life. Pay closer attention to what fulfills you and "wash your hands" of any issues that might be holding you back from your full potential.

What Freud Would Say: Although Freud did not analyze dreams of hands per se, it's clear that he would have interpreted images of prominent hands, and especially fingers, as phallic symbols. He also endorsed the dubious ethical equation, first advanced in the work of psychoanalyst Wilhelm Stekel, that in dream symbolism, all things "right" (including being right-handed) represent the path of righteousness, correctness, and, interestingly, heterosexuality; and that all things "left" (including being left-handed) instead represent crime, perversion, and homosexuality.

What Jung Would Say:

Author Sandra Thomson says that Jungian analysts routinely attribute right-hand dream imagery to masculine or active qualities and left-hand dream imagery to feminine or passive qualities—an interesting counterpoint to Freud. And Jung, in his book *Dreams*, equated the right side (and right hand) with conscious behavior and the left side (and left hand) with the unconscious.

Cultural Context:

In religious symbolism, the hand represents not personal ambition but divine will—the "hand of God" as absolute power and an instrument of fate. The practice of palmistry—divining someone's personality and future activity by "reading" the lines and bumps on the palm of the hand (as well as the shape and texture of the hand itself)—dates back to Greek mythology, when each finger and area of the hand related to a specific god and the issues or talents associated with that god. Palmistry and other types of oracular divination often employ a "third eye" symbol in the center of the palm—a mystical image that simultaneously conveys omniscience (the all-seeing eye) and omnipotence (the all-powerful hand). This image appears in religious art of the Aztecs, Native Americans, Hindus, Muslims, and Hebrews, among others. When the hand appears by itself, fingers pointed down, it's called a *hamsa*, a talisman common to many Middle Eastern and Mediterranean cultures, thought to protect the bearer from the "evil eye."

Related Images: Brain (p. 39); Connections, Missed (p. 61); Ears (p. 87); Eyes (p. 103); The Impossible Task (p. 140); Paralysis/Running in Slow Motion (p. 178)

41. **FIRE/BEING BURNED**

Common Manifestations: Dreams of fire can be intense and disturbing. You might dream that a wildfire streaks across the landscape, out of control and headed straight for you. Or you could dream of watching your home—past or present—go up in a blaze. Are you the one who started the fire, or do you frantically try to extinguish it? Fire dreams can also be strangely hypnotic; perhaps in the dream you are staring, mesmerized, at a controlled flame—in a fireplace or emanating from a group of candles.

Variations: A related aspect of fire dreams is to imagine that you or someone you know and love has been burned—accidentally or purposefully, perhaps as torture or punishment. Burning at the stake is another illustration of this idea, as is being immolated on a funeral pyre or being forced to walk across a bed of hot lava.

Occurrence:

Dreams of fire often occur in menopausal women, according to psychologist Alan Siegel, who has devoted his career to studying how life experiences and rites of passage shape a person's dreams. Siegel also found that AIDS and cancer patients sometimes dream of wildfires spreading across large patches of land.

The Spin:

One of the four primary elements (along with water, air, and earth), fire is a masculine, aggressive symbol that usually represents the spirit or energy. It conveys passion (a "fiery" personality), rage ("burning" with anger), and intensity (*fire* is a jeweler's term used to gauge a diamond's brilliance). Fire can destroy, but it also has the power to transform and purify all that it encounters.

???

Assuming the imagery is metaphoric and not a posttraumatic reenactment of a waking-life experience, go back to your dream and think for a moment how you felt when faced with the blaze. Were you relieved to have the material world obliterated, forcing you to start anew? You might be yearning for just that kind of clean break from the stresses of your everyday waking life. Were you terrified of how quickly the fire engulfed you? Perhaps anger simmers close to your emotional surface, and you fear it will burn out of control. Did you work to put the fire out? If so, your dream firefighter might be trying to keep a lid on your passion. If the fire consumed you, perhaps you're simply a slave to your desires. Remember the legend of the phoenix, the mythological Egyptian bird that represented both death and resurrection. At the end of five hundred years, the phoenix immolated itself by fire, only to be reborn from the ashes of its corpse. It's a nice commentary on the circular nature ("ashes to ashes") and persistence of life. No matter how many mistakes you make, life does go on.

Hypnotic dreams of staring into a flame could indicate a journey toward enlightenment or self-knowledge—as long as the dream fire is more illuminating than destructive. Being burned, on the other hand, could be a message of guilt that your unconscious needs to exorcise. You might feel the urge to torture or punish yourself for some action you've taken or behavior you've exhibited in waking life. If the person being burned in the dream is you, perhaps you're trying to purge yourself of unpleasant or destructive thoughts. If someone else is being burned, comb through the dream clues to pinpoint who or what that person represents. Is the sacrificial victim a job that has "burned you out"? A person you trusted who betrayed you? Maybe it's an aspect of your own personality that you're neglecting or suppressing.

What Freud Would Say:
In two works, *The Interpretation of Dreams* and *Fragment of an Analysis of a Case of Hysteria*, Freud addressed a fire dream relayed by Dora, one of his patients. After analyzing her at length, Freud concluded that the dream of fire pointed to a recollection of

childhood episodes of bed-wetting. He claimed his interpretation "justifies the nursery law which forbids a child to 'play with fire'—so that he shall not wet his bed at night." This smells like one of Freud's famous dream reversals.

What Jung Would Say:

Jung, as a student of alchemy, felt that the presence of fire in dreams often heralded some kind of transformation (much as alchemists employed fire in attempts to transform base metals into gold) or, more likely, spiritual awakening. He supported the latter theory by citing both George Bernard Shaw's play *Saint Joan* ("The fire that is not put out is a holy fire") and apocryphal Christian scripture ("The Savior himself says: He that is near me is near the fire").

Cultural Context:

In the same way that walking on broken glass (p. 126) is considered an exercise of iron will and mental discipline, so is the mystical practice of firewalking. Tribal elders and shamans in the indigenous cultures of Africa, Asia, the Americas, and the Pacific Islands practiced firewalking as a form of prayer, to induce visions and ritually cleanse the community. Meditating until they enter a trancelike state, firewalkers are said to use their minds to alter the perception of reality; if they do not believe they will be burned, they won't be burned—though the hot coals reach temperatures of nine hundred degrees Fahrenheit (482°C) and beyond. Such an extreme example of mind over matter seems to defy logic—one of the reasons this practice takes on an almost dreamlike quality. Latter-day firewalkers pursue the ritual as a way to face their fears and empower other areas of their lives.

Related Images: Crime, Victim of (p. 70); Glass, Broken (p. 126); Home, Childhood (p. 136)

42. **FLYING**

Common Manifestations:
In the "good" flying dream, the setting is immaterial. The salient feature is that you suddenly have the power of flight (not as pilot or passenger—more like a superhero). You soar into the air, unfettered, with an intoxicating sense of freedom. Once airborne, you realize how easy it is to steer and navigate, and so you focus on enjoying the scenery around you.

Variations:
In the "bad" flying dream, you struggle to get off the ground or are unable to stay in the air. Perhaps you are forced into flight to escape something unpleasant— a bad situation, a crisis, or a dangerous person.

Occurrence:
This dream arises most often in youth, but crops up from time to time after reaching adulthood.

The Spin:
When it's good, it's good, but when it's bad, it can be terrifying. The happy flying dream is one of the few

that is unequivocally positive. You're feeling proud for something you've accomplished or created in your life, and your dream self takes flight in celebration. So lie back and enjoy it. The only potential down side is that "pride" might edge into "full of yourself" or "superiority" if you're not careful.

???

If your flying dream is fraught with failure and insecurity, your unconscious may be trying to alert you that something blocks your progress. Is a particular person, emotion, or relationship weighing you down? If, instead, you're flying to escape a threat, perhaps you're avoiding a problem that needs attention. Try to pinpoint what in the dream you're fleeing from and whether those circumstances have a parallel in your waking life.

What Freud Would Say: Flying dreams hearken back to childhood, when swinging, seesawing, and sliding evoked pleasurable feelings. But even innocent shenanigans such as these have sexual overtones, and therefore can properly be understood as a disguised expression of sexual desire. In men, flying dreams often trigger erections; in women, the dreams hint at the unconscious wish to be a man.

What Jung Would Say: Flying signifies the achievement of a higher consciousness, the ability to free yourself of the things that hold you back.

Cultural
Context:

The prospect of flight has fascinated mankind for thousands of years, long before the Wright brothers built their first airplane. According to psychologist Gayle Delaney, the Greek dream expert Artemidorus wrote in 200 CE that the higher the dream flight, the more prosperity and good fortune for the dreamer. Flying also signified freedom for slaves and money for the poor. Many ancient and tribal societies felt that the dream self actually conducted a thriving out-of-body existence, leaving the physical self behind during sleep to travel great distances through other worlds in search of wisdom and enlightenment. Members of Aboriginal tribes of Australia and New Zealand and Native American tribes of North America rigorously practiced fasting and isolation in order to prompt more vivid, authentic dream states.

Related Images: Airplane (p. 11); Chased, Being (p. 48)

43.   **GLASS, BROKEN**

Common
Manifestations:

In your dream, you are walking barefoot over razor-sharp shards of broken glass, crying out in pain. Or perhaps you are compelled to ingest the glass, chewing and swallowing with great difficulty. However you encounter the glass, it slices into you like scores of sharp little knives, drawing blood.

Variations: The dream glass might crop up unexpectedly—for
               example, in a dream of walking into or falling through
               a completely transparent plate-glass window that rains
               daggers of broken glass all around you.

The Spin: The sharp, slicing nature of broken glass often serves
    as a metaphor for hurtful words or "shattering" expe-
               riences. Did something in your life break or fall apart,
               wounding you in the process? In walking across the
               broken glass, you are traversing a path of pain, which
               might mirror a waking-life struggle you encounter
               every morning when you open your eyes. If you dream
               of eating pieces of glass, perhaps you are "swallowing"
               the pain in your life, keeping the hurt locked inside.
               Or, external forces are asking you to "digest" something
               unpleasant in reality. The highly charged image of
               glass shards—promising both pain and bloodshed—
               indicates that the root cause or association is an
               emotional one, probably relating to a love or family
               relationship. Your unconscious has chosen the poetic,
               if intense, imagery of broken glass to dramatize your
               pain and prompt you toward change, for the sake
               of well-being.

    Walking into a plate-glass window that shatters all
               around you could illustrate a sudden, wrenching life
               awakening. An obstacle that you didn't realize was there
               (a sheet of glass, of course, is transparent) suddenly
               blocks your path; by shattering, it causes unexpected,
               sweeping pain. Curiously, however, there might be an

up side to this dream. Psychologist and author Sandra Thomson posits that glass often represents the emotional walls people erect to repress thoughts and feelings. So in the dream, if you purposefully break the glass, you may be trying to approach life with a newfound openness and peace.

If Recurrent:

⚠

It's possible you are repressing some serious pain; it's healthiest in the long run if you acknowledge and address it as soon as you can.

What Freud Would Say:

Although Freud did not deconstruct dreams of broken glass specifically, in his 1901 work *Psychopathology of Everyday Life* he devoted a chapter to something he called "Erroneously Carried-Out Actions"—clumsy or accidental waking-life mishaps. Not surprisingly, he argued that dropping a glass or breaking an object of some value is never accidental or unintentional; it always represents the attempt to fulfill an unconscious wish—the wish being whatever effect, positive or negative, the breaking might have.

What Jung Would Say:

Jung also did not specifically analyze dreams of broken glass, but in his writing he alluded to a glass container as a powerful dream symbol. Jung was drawn to the language and mysticism of alchemy, the medieval philosophy centered on finding a method for transforming base metals into gold. Jung equated the alchemists' search for gold with each individual's search for the

Self. He believed that, in dreams, any glass receptacle symbolized the *unum vas*, an egg-shaped vessel alchemists used in their metallurgic experiments to "cook" various combinations of materials in search of that one timeless formula. And for Jung, this medieval experimental process directly paralleled the rigorous self-analysis necessary to achieve individuation, the highest level of consciousness.

Cultural Context:

Broken glass may be a dream image that induces pain in the dreamer, but in waking life, some use it as the ultimate triumph of mind over matter. For hundreds of years, certain people who are advanced on the path of spiritual enlightenment or physical discipline—yogis, Sufis, mystics, martial arts masters, and others—have demonstrated the ability to enter a trancelike state and walk barefoot across large beds of razor-sharp broken glass without pain, and without injury to the feet. Practitioners claim it has a reflexology effect, to stimulate the body's pressure points, and that it also allows them to face and conquer their fears.

Related Images: Falling (p. 107); Fire/Being Burned (p. 120)

44. **HAIR**

Common Manifestations:

Something unusual has happened to your hair; perhaps you've asked for, or inadvertently received, a weird haircut. Maybe you have dreamed that your hair is falling out. Conversely, the hair in your dream may be growing at an alarming rate. Hair dreams—at least when they don't involve going bald—often have strong sensual overtones.

The Spin:

As something that sprouts from the head, hair can symbolize our thoughts and intellect, and it is a metaphor for overall health and vitality. Dreams of long hair, especially if you have short hair, can indicate a willingness to get in touch with your sensual side, just as losing hair or going bald can hint at a loss of strength or sexual potency. The state of your hair in the dream often serves as an internal barometer. Wild or disheveled hair can reflect disorganized or confused thoughts. Similarly, dream haircuts may represent an attempt you're making in waking life to effect change. According to dream expert Jeremy Taylor, "Whenever odd things having to do with hair show up in the dream world, it's always worth asking the question: 'How do these images of hair symbolize my changing thoughts and opinions?'"

If Recurrent:

You might be struggling to break out of old habits and learn a new way of looking at life and its challenges.

What Freud Would Say:

In *The Interpretation of Dreams*, Freud stated that the presence of animal fur in dreams is a veiled symbol for pubic hair.

What Jung Would Say:	According to the Jungian dream interpretation Web site mythsdreamssymbols.com, dreaming of getting a haircut may speak to your unconscious feelings of being judged or censored by someone in your life. Dreaming that your hair is very long may mean that you are thinking "long" and hard about making a big decision in your life. Losing your hair in a dream could address feelings of powerlessness in a particular situation. And dreaming that your hair has turned gray or white may signal the recent acquisition of profound wisdom.
Cultural Context:	These particular dream associations have a long, vivid history. Copious hair has long been associated with virility—an association that dates back to the book of Judges in the Old Testament. Judges tells the story of Samson, appointed by God to lead Israel. As a member of the Nazarite sect of Judaism, he showed his religious devotion by refusing to cut his hair. God granted him superhuman powers; Samson famously killed a lion with his bare hands and slew a thousand Philistines with the jawbone of an ass. Samson also had a thing for exotic women—his ultimate downfall. He fell in love with Delilah, a Philistine who betrayed him by revealing the secret of his strength: his long hair. She arranged to have his hair cut off while he slept, and afterward, authorities captured him and gouged his eyes out. Ultimately, Samson's hair grew back in jail, and although permanently blind, he was able to

destroy the Philistine rulers. In this way, biblical scholars point out, Samson's strong faith in God overcame his human shortcomings.

Related Images: Brain (p. 39); Mouth and Teeth (p. 166); Teeth Falling Out (p. 219)

---

45. **HEART**

Common Manifestations: There's something wrong with your heart. Perhaps you're feeling chest pain or palpitations, or your heart is beating so fast—with fear or desire—that you worry you might pass out. You might even dream of undergoing heart surgery.

Variations: You might also have a dream in which your heart, or the heart of someone you love, is much larger than it normally should be.

The Spin: The heart as the common cultural symbol for romantic love indicates that dreams involving your physical heart could provide clues to the way you deal with your feelings. What is your approach to relationships— do you wear your heart on your sleeve or play it close to the vest? Do you give your heart away easily, or has a past heartbreak closed you off and made you more reluctant to reach out? Dreams of heart trouble don't have to refer to a love match—it could also refer to doubts or fears you have over being true to yourself. Have you "followed your heart" in your education or career? Do you have the emotional strength to handle the hurdles you face in your life? Perhaps dreaming of a weak heart indicates a lack of resiliency in responding to stressful life events.

If Recurrent:

It's possible, though admittedly not likely, that multiple or repeated dreams of heart trouble could be your unconscious hinting at the onset of an illness.

What Freud Would Say:

In *The Interpretation of Dreams*, Freud took issue with the kind of strictly symbolic imagery that equated dreams of a house and its rooms with parts of the human body. He specifically cited the writings of late nineteenth-century psychologist Karl Scherner, who argued that body parts such as the lungs were represented in dreams by a "blazing furnace" and the heart by "hollow boxes or baskets."

Cultural Context:

The heart has long been viewed as the seat of emotion, despite the fact that modern science locates the generation and processing of emotions in the amygdalae, two almond-shaped groupings of cells in the brain. Scriptural references as far back as the Egyptian Book of the Dead and the Old Testament refer to "having heart," essentially meaning pure motives and divine grace. Interestingly, the Babylonians believed the heart to be the seat of the intellect and the liver to be the seat of passion and emotion—a theory shared by classical philosophers such as Aristotle and Galen. Some historians speculate that the common heart shape (♡) dates back to an ancient Sumerian symbol for woman, a shape with sexual connotations that could resemble either female breasts, buttocks, or the pubic area.

Related Images: Brain (p. 39); Liver (p. 153)

HISTORICAL FIGURES

Common
Manifestations:

In this dream, you are witness to history. Have you traveled back in time to see a momentous event unfold—Washington crossing the Delaware or the fall of the Berlin Wall? Maybe you're having a little one-on-one time with a world figure—taking tea with Churchill, or advising Cleopatra on matters of the heart. What matters is that this is your date with destiny.

The Spin:

To dream of historical figures is to give your ideals a human guise. The first step in decoding this dream is to determine what the historical figure means to you—nobility? Vision? Grace under pressure? A fierce, never-say-die spirit? Often, the traits you most admire in this historical figure are traits you'd like to assume yourself, or traits you harbor but have not yet acknowledged. Dream dictionary author Sandra Thomson believes that historical figures often represent feelings from your past that need reconciliation.

If Recurrent: You might want to register that time-travel machine for a patent.

What Freud
Would Say: Freud analyzed dreams of and about historical persons, but didn't ascribe a meaning to the characters in the dream—only the content.

What Jung
Would Say: According to the Jungian dream analysis Web site mythsdreamssymbols.com, famous people who turn up in dreams often represent qualities to which you aspire, or qualities in your personality that you have not yet acknowledged in your conscious mind. In this way, the dream figure may correspond to your Shadow archetype, or may represent particular aspects of your Persona.

Cultural
Context: If you had the chance to travel back in time, would you use the opportunity to meet famous historical figures? Definitely, especially if it was the only way to earn a passing grade in history. That's the premise behind the 1989 movie *Bill & Ted's Excellent Adventure*, in which Keanu Reeves and Alex Winter portray clueless teens who climb into a magic phone booth and hurtle into the past to gather "personages of historical significance" for a most impressive multimedia oral exam. Among the people they introduce to twentieth-century life are Socrates (pronounced "SOH-craytes" by

this duo), Napoleon, Genghis Khan, Joan of Arc, Abraham Lincoln, and none other than the father of psychoanalysis himself, Sigmund Freud ("But you can call me Siggy").

Related Images: Biblical Figures and Religious Icons (p. 34); Celebrities (p. 46)

47. 📷   **HOME, CHILDHOOD**

Common
Manifestations: You're walking through a house you immediately rec- ognize as one from your childhood. This is where you grew up, vividly recreated down to the very last knick- knack. You might be there as an omniscient observer, watching your child self interacting with other members of your family. Or, you could be walking through the home in your grown-up guise, your adult self inter- acting with people from your past.

The Spin: The house is a very personal, immediate dream symbol,
💡 💙 ???   one which can evoke a specific time in someone's life, but which can also serve as a metaphor for the self. Many psychologists extend the metaphor of house-as- self to state that a dream of your parents' house indicates an emotional regression toward childhood. But such a simplistic statement ignores the psyche's many nuances. Certainly dreaming of a childhood home alludes to your feelings about your mother and

father. But why have this dream now? What positive or negative memories are associated with that house, with that time of your life? Do any situations from that period relate to something happening right now? Your mind chose to travel to that period for a reason— most likely, to illuminate a situation or problem you're currently facing. Understanding the connection between your dream past and your waking present could shed light on recurring emotional baggage and prevent history from repeating itself.

What Freud Would Say:	Freud devoted an entire section of *The Interpretation of Dreams* to what he called "infantile material as the source of dreams." For Freud, wish-fulfillment dreams that formed out of acknowledged and repressed child-hood memories were the most common—and potentially the most illuminating—types of dreams. Even in assessing his own dreams, Freud said, "In the latent content of a dream I come unexpectedly upon a scene from childhood, and . . . all at once a whole series of my dreams link up with the associations branching out from some experience of my childhood."
What Jung Would Say:	The house is a metaphor for the Self—Jung famously referred to the house as the "mansion of the soul." In analyzing regressive dreams of youth, Jung stated, "Return to childhood is always the return to the father and mother . . . with [childhood's] long and momentous history."

Cultural Context:

The notion that recalling a past event can shed light on one's life in the here and now has been fodder not just for dreams, but for literature as well. Perhaps the most famous example is Marcel Proust's epic seven-volume work *À la recherche du temps perdu* (originally translated as *Remembrance of Things Past* but now more commonly referred to as *In Search of Lost Time*). In the book's first volume, the fictional narrator (some say a thinly veiled version of Proust himself) tastes a madeleine dipped in tea and is immediately, and vividly, transported to a time in his childhood when he enjoyed the same cake and tea while visiting his great-aunt at the family country home. This powerful sense memory triggers an extended flashback that recounts the story of the narrator's life. The ideological thread that runs throughout Proust's entire work is that we are what we remember, and those memories, our life experiences, are the base material from which all art is fashioned.

Related Images: Attic (p. 24); Basement (p. 26); Corridors/Hallways (p. 64); Kitchen (p. 151); Rooms, Secret (p. 199); Rooms, Unused (p. 202)

48. **HOSPITAL**

Common Manifestations:

You're in the hospital, for reasons that may not be entirely clear. However, you hear the beeping of the

Color Plates

Icon Key

childhood or adolescence	adulthood	old age
female	male	

THE SPIN

happiness	sadness	illness
love	heartbreak	sex

THE SPIN (continued)		
death	success	fame
uncertainty	conflict	epiphany

CONTEXT			
biology	literature	film	television

MISCELLANEOUS		
caution	illustration	

1a. **accident with train**

1b. **accident with car**

2a. **airplane travel**

2b. **airplane disaster**

3. **aliens**

4. angels

5. animal, attack by wild

6a. **animals, exotic**

6b. **animals, domestic**

7. **attic**

8. **basement**

9. beach/ocean

10. bed, something under

11a. **biblical figures**

11b. **religious icons**

12. **boat**

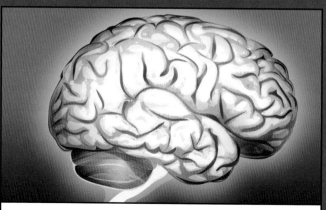

13. **brain**

14. **car trouble**

15. **cave**

16a. **celebrities:** on red carpet

16b. **celebrities:** madonna in everyday life

17. **chased, being**

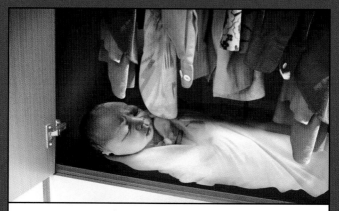

18a. **child, discovering**

18b. **child, forgetting or misplacing**

19. **city**

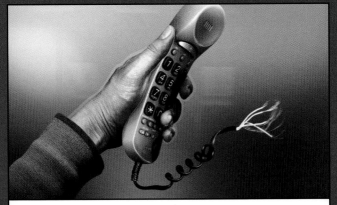

20. **communication breakdown**

21. **computers**

22. **connections, missed**

23a. **corridors/hallways**

23b. **staircases, endless**

24. **crime, committing**

25. **crime, victim of**

26. **death of loved one (unrelated to actual death)**

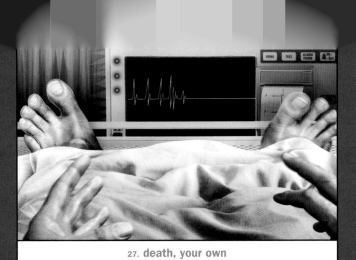

27. **death, your own**

28. **deceased loved one, visit from**

29a. **desert island, peaceful**

29b. **desert island, sinister**

30. **drowning/breathing underwater**

31. **ears**

32. **elevators**

33. **elimination, inappropriate or inconvenient**

34. **end of the world**

35a. **public performance**

35b. **exam**

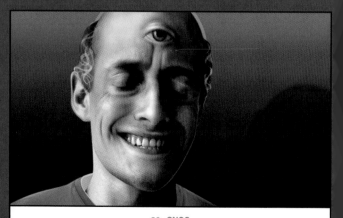

36. **eyes**

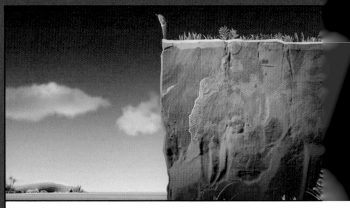

37. falling

38. father

39a. **feet, legs, and shoes**

39b. **footprints**

40. **fingers and hands**

41. **fire/being burned**

42. **flying**

43. **glass, broken**

44a. **hair, abundant**

44b. **hair loss**

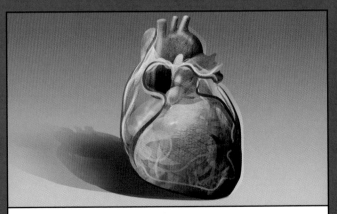

45. **heart**

46a. historical figures: advising cleopatra

46b. historical figures: tea with churchill

47. home, childhood

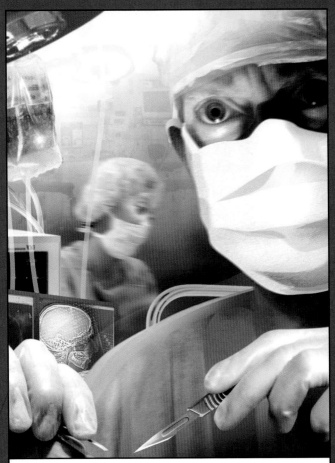

48. **hospital**

49. **the impossible task**

50. **infidelity**

51a. **insects, infestation**

51b. **insects, appealing**

52. **jungle**

53. **kitchen**

54. **liver**

55. **lost, being**

56. **mechanical malfunction**

57. **monsters**

58. mother

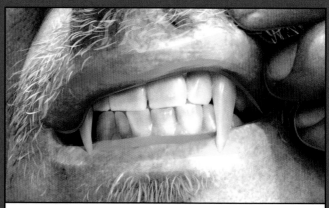

59. mouth and teeth

60. **mud**

61. **natural disasters: earthquakes, tornadoes, and volcanoes**

62. nudity, public

63. **paralysis/running in slow motion**

64. **partner/spouse**

65. **police officers**

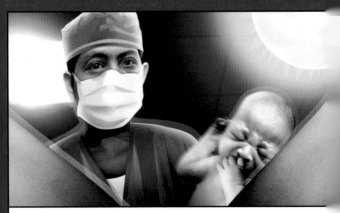

66. **pregnancy/giving birth**

67. prison

68. purse or wallet, lost

69. rain

70. **rivers**

71. **rooms, secret**

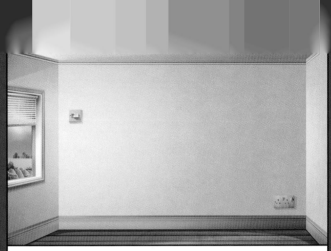

72. **rooms, unused**

73. **sex, gender reversal**

74. **sex interrupted**

75. **sex in public**

76. **sex with someone you know (not your partner)**

77. **sex with stranger/ghost**

78. **swamp**

79. **teeth falling out**

80. **treasure, buried**

81. **tunnel**

82a. **vehicle that isn't a vehicle:** illogical mode of transportation

82b. **vehicle that isn't a vehicle:** illogical use of vehicle

83. **war zone**

84. **water**

85. weapons: guns and knives

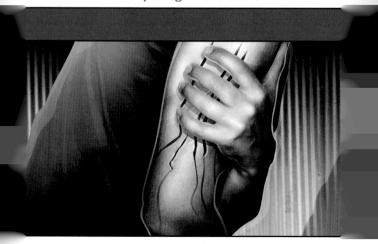

86. wounds

monitors, you can smell the antiseptic, and you are being poked and prodded by various doctors and nurses. Depending on the nature of your dream malady, this might not be an entirely unpleasant experience.

Occurrence: This dream may arise at times of significant stress or personal unhappiness in your life.

The Spin: Hospitals are where we go when we face a physical problem that's outside our control—when we need help to heal. The dream may express a rather concrete anxiety about a planned medical procedure. But it's not hard to extend this metaphor into the emotional or even spiritual realm; in your waking life, perhaps you're feeling overwhelmed and need to "check out" for a little while and attend to your own well-being. This could be an indication that you need support and pampering from those around you, or it could be a sign that you need to learn to take better care of yourself. Dream dictionary author Sandra Thomson recommends scrutinizing the symbolism of any specifically injured body parts for additional meaning.

If Recurrent: It might be time to schedule your annual physical.

What Jung Would Say: Jung viewed hospital dream images as calls for internal reconciliation—signs that the conscious and unconscious minds need patience, understanding, and acceptance to find balance and continue along the road to individuation.

Cultural Context:

Medical care and spiritual nourishment have been linked for centuries. Egyptian and Greek temples were the first documented places of healing—sick people would make a pilgrimage to the closest temple and encamp there while waiting for a vision from the gods with advice on how to heal. After the widespread advent of Christianity, treating the sick became the province of religious clerics, and Europe's early hospitals were administered by monks and nuns. In the Middle Ages, hospitals also provided for the poor and housed religious pilgrims, enforcing the link between medical treatment and compassion and providing a tangible etymology for the word *hospitality*.

Related Images:

Death of Loved One (Unrelated to Actual Death) (p. 73); Death, Your Own (p. 76); Pregnancy/Giving Birth (p. 187)

49. **THE IMPOSSIBLE TASK**

Common Manifestations:

Your dream is a no-win situation, pure and simple. Perhaps you have to bail out a sinking boat with a broken teacup, or scale a wall that grows higher with every bit you climb, or complete an obstacle course that gets more and more treacherous as you go. What do all of these images have in common? Your dreaming mind has deliberately constructed the scenario to be unachievable—and the harder you try, the more difficult and improbable your success becomes.

The Spin:

This dream gives voice to your frustration. In your waking life, you're probably feeling caught up in something—a bureaucratic job, a dead-end relationship, an emotionally fraught family bond—that just isn't working. Take a moment to appreciate how this dream is actually a gift from your unconscious. It's sending you the message to stop beating your head against a wall and try a new approach. It's clear that the way you have been tackling this challenge has just not been effective.

If Recurrent:

You are wedded to a fixed way of thinking, and it's holding you back. Take a deep breath and try approaching your dilemmas (or bad habits) from another angle. Sometimes, simply looking at the same old situation in a different light can provide valuable insight.

What Freud Would Say:

Freud called these types of dreams punishment dreams, which arose out of the mind's masochistic impulses. He actually felt these were most common at times when one's waking life was quite successful, another example of what he called dream reversals. In some cases, Freud also felt the inability to achieve a certain task expressed an unconscious fear of impotence.

What Jung Would Say:	Dreams of frustration could signify an emotional disturbance or conflict within the psyche—between the conscious and unconscious minds, or between such opposing internal forces as masculine and feminine or aggression and passivity.
Cultural Context:	"Outside the box" thinking—finding new, nimble ways to address and resolve seemingly impossible problems—has long been regarded a barometer of intelligence and wisdom. History points to great thinkers as those who questioned the things everyone else took for granted. Galileo and Copernicus asked, what if the Earth is not the center of the universe? Edison, who had no formal education, wondered how best to harness electricity for reliable, widespread indoor use. And Einstein dug even deeper, approaching the very fabric of time and space with curiosity.
Related Images:	Teeth Falling Out (p. 219)

50. **INFIDELITY**

Common Manifestations:	You dream that your partner is cheating on you. Perhaps you walk in on the troubling scene, or your partner confesses the transgression, or someone else in your life breaks the bad news to you. Regardless of how your dream conveys the information, the discovery is devastating.

Variations: You dream that you are the one cheating on your partner. For more on this type of dream, see "Sex with Stranger," p. 215, or "Sex with Someone You Know (Not Your Partner)," p. 211.

Occurrence: Though it might seem illogical, infidelity dreams often arise once you are in a stable, monogamous relationship.

The Spin: The obvious worry is that such an infidelity dream is prophetic, and your unconscious is trying to bring a suspicion out into the open. Certainly this is a possibility. But ask yourself honestly if reality supports this interpretation. Do you really think your significant other has a thing on the side? Or do you feel neglected for some other reason—maybe your spouse or partner spends less time and energy on you than on friends, work, or some other passion (the "sports widow" syndrome).

More often, this type of dream magnifies the anxiety you feel at the prospect of losing someone you love. Once you enter into a stable relationship—and certainly if you've started a family—you have more to lose, and so your mind is preoccupied with how to hold on to what you have.

If Recurrent: Talk to your partner about scheduling some "you time." You might also consider taking up a hobby of your own. Or hire a private investigator with a good telephoto lens.

What Freud Would Say:	Freud believed that the unconscious mind used dreams to express secret wishes, but that in the process of remembering these dreams upon waking, the mind often distorted the nature of those wishes. So in discussing the dream with a patient, he often conducted what he called reversals—understanding a dream symbol as the embodiment of its opposite. In this way, for Freud, dreaming of a partner's infidelity could indicate your unconscious desire to have an adulterous relationship yourself.
What Jung Would Say:	Relationship dreams often follow one of two interpretations. They can refer quite directly to your real-life partnership. Metaphorically, such dreams may also speak to the union (or disunion) of the different parts of your psyche. If you are troubled by dreams of adultery, perhaps you are insecure about the strength of your current relationship. Or, your subconscious could be sending the message that you're not being true to yourself, that the things on which you spend time and energy are keeping you out of balance.
Cultural Context:	Infidelity has been a sin since the days of the Tenth Commandment ("Thou shalt not covet thy neighbor's wife"). Although the Old Testament books of Deuteronomy and Leviticus stipulate that the punishment for adultery should be death for both perpetrators, it cannot escape attention that women who commit infidelity have been judged more harshly throughout

history. In certain conservative Islamic societies, women suspected of fornication outside the marriage bond can be either flogged or sentenced to *rajm* (death by stoning)—but some scholars question whether such a punishment is specifically outlined in the Qur'an.

Fictionally, Shakespeare's Othello may not have dreamt of his wife's infidelity, but the false, scurrilous aspersions that Iago cast upon Desdemona's virtue so tormented Othello that he murdered her and then, realizing his mistake, killed himself. In Nathaniel Hawthorne's *The Scarlet Letter*, townspeople force Hester Prynne to wear a scarlet *A* pinned to her breast to symbolize her adultery. But in taking responsibility for her behavior, she makes peace with it and moves on. In contrast, the devoutly religious man with whom Hester bore an out-of-wedlock child, Arthur Dimmesdale, never revealed the affair (or his paternity) and was so guilt-striken by harboring the secret that he became ill. At the end of the novel, he dies in Hester's arms, finally confessing his sin to the townspeople and finding a measure of relief.

Related Images: Sex with Someone You Know (Not Your Partner) (p. 211); Sex with Stranger (p. 215)

51. **INSECTS**

Common Manifestations:

Among the dreams with a high gross-out factor are those that feature insects. They could be pestilent in nature—your apartment is overcome with roaches, or ants threaten your picnic. Or, the dream could take a sinister turn into movie-of-the-week material: Swarms of bees chase you down the street, or basketball-sized, biting spiders prowl the hallways of your home, looking for a tasty snack. The common thread in this dream is the single-mindedness of the infestation, either in terms of the sheer number or the intimidating size of the insects. You wake up with your skin crawling.

Variations: The dream could be somewhat more pleasant—perhaps you're watching thousands of colorful butterflies alight from branches.

The Spin: Insects, like dream images of animals (p. 21), are obvious metaphors for the specific traits and unconscious urges inside all of us—and those traits could range from the mundane (an antlike work ethic) to the disturbing (the desire to trap your competition in a web you've spun around them). The more aggressive the insect invasion in your dream, the more powerful and instinctual the urge. A single, persistent insect could symbolize a problem that has dogged you for a while.

Specific insects hold different meanings for different people. Entomologists and beekeepers, for example, will no doubt ascribe radically different meanings to their insect dreams than will a young child terrified by creepy crawlies. What is the character of the particular insect in your dream, and does it correspond to anyone's behavior you have witnessed in your waking life? Painting in broad strokes, bees and ants are communal creatures, cogs in a complicated machine that work toward a single goal (is that how you see yourself in relation to your work?). Roaches symbolize filth but also have an admirable, post-apocalyptic kind of tenacity. Butterflies enact an almost mystical transformation from coarse, plodding caterpillars into gorgeous, floating, ethereal creatures. And spiders, often associated with wisdom and known for spinning elaborate, delicate webs, receive nourishment by devouring those around them. Do you feel trapped in someone's web of deceit?

What Freud Would Say:	In *The Interpretation of Dreams*, Freud stated that "being plagued with vermin is often a sign of pregnancy." In later years he also argued that spiders were dream manifestations of a devouring mother figure.
What Jung Would Say:	Jung wrote at great length about wild creatures, each with its own mythic and cultural symbolism. As a phenomenon, however, he considered them dream archetypes of the Shadow self—symbols of the mysteries of the unconscious mind, or what he called the dark center. According to Jungian dream analyst Jeremy Taylor, the more ominous or life-threatening the dream encounter, the more likely that the dreamer is disconnected from his intuitions and instincts in waking life. But Taylor also asserts that remembering

the dream is a positive indication that the dreamer intends to tackle these issues, at least on some level.

Cultural Context:
Interestingly, the word *psyche* translates from the ancient Greek as both "butterfly" and "soul." Spider deities were revered in several Native American cultures. The Lakota tell of a trickster spider god named Iktomi who spun webs of deceit among gods and humans alike. The Navajo speak of a powerful goddess called the Spider Grandmother, the source of all creation, who spins a web across the sky that links all peoples and civilizations. Both Iktomi and the Spider Grandmother are tied to the cultural symbolism of the Native American dream catcher, a talisman said to keep nightmares at bay. The catcher is made of a wooden hoop decorated with feathers and beads that frames a net representing the spider god's web.

Related Images:
Animals (p. 21); Chased, Being (p. 48); Monsters (p. 160); Paralysis/Running in Slow Motion (p. 178)

52. **JUNGLE**

Common Manifestations:
You are wandering through the jungle, uneasy and lost and overwhelmed by sensory input. Dense foliage, bright colors, and humidity surround you. In such a crowded environment you lose geographic perspective (it's hard to see more than an arm's length in front of

you), but your ears fill with the sounds of wildlife—insects buzzing, birds calling, monkeys screeching. However, you can't shake the ominous feeling that other wild animals are padding through the jungle, watching you, camouflaged by the greenery and waiting for the right moment to strike.

Occurrence: People in high-pressure careers often report intense jungle dreams.

The Spin: The jungle is a dream image that evokes primitive feelings of aggression and survival. Being stuck in a jungle is at once frightening (what's hiding in the bushes, ready to pounce?) and claustrophobic (the flora closes in, from the sides and on the top, until you can't even see the sun). Assess whether, in your waking life, you face a similarly hostile, primordial environment. In most cases, this is a dream metaphor for the stress and competition you face every day at work—a place teeming with people who watch your every move and wait for the chance to capitalize on your weakness (a concrete jungle, as it were). Your path is often unclear, and yet, despite fear and setbacks, you soldier on. If, in the dream, you cultivate the skills necessary to defend yourself and hack your way through the brush and back to civilization, it's a good sign that you have the spirit and the ambition necessary to weather any challenges to your authority in the working world.

If Recurrent:	Perhaps it's time to check out of the rat race—or at the very least, reconsider a career choice that forces you to ponder betrayal and look over your shoulder at every waking moment.
What Freud Would Say:	One of the central principles of Freud's psychoanalytic theory was that aggression is a primary motivation for human behavior. In *The Interpretation of Dreams*, he argued that "wild beasts, as a rule, are employed by the dream-work to represent passionate impulses of which the dreamer is afraid, whether they are his own or of other people." But Freud believed that because unconscious aggression evokes such guilt and fear in the conscious mind, the dreamer automatically "separated off his neurosis" and depicted it as a separate entity—in this case, the wild animals that wait to attack the person stuck in the jungle.
What Jung Would Say:	In his writing, Jung often referred to a "primeval forest" inhabited by snakes, apes, and other wild animals. For Jung, this was a symbol of the unconscious, and, like Freud, he believed the wildness found within this dream setting represented instincts and aggressions about which the dreamer felt fear or guilt.
Cultural Context:	Although the jungle symbolizes nature in a kind of original, untainted state, it also serves as a metaphor for modern civilization taken to a competitive extreme. That disconnect—between the primitive wild of the

jungle and the equally dangerous pitfalls of "civilized" society—is a common theme in books and cinema. The well-worn tale of the child raised by wild animals dates as far back as the *Epic of Gilgamesh* in ancient Babylonia; Roman mythology relates the tale of the twins, Romulus and Remus, who were raised by wolves and went on to found the city of Rome. Modern examples would be Mowgli in Rudyard Kipling's *The Jungle Book* and the title character of Edgar Rice Burroughs's Tarzan novels. What these stories have in common is the naïve notion that children raised apart from civilization carry the distilled, uncorrupted essence of humanity, with the intelligence of humanity but the skill, strength, and guilelessness of an animal. Contemporary critics now view both Kipling and Burroughs as advocates for the racist, paternalistic views of their time, in which the white man—even one raised by "animals"—is meant to reign over the jungle and its "native" inhabitants.

Related Images: Animals (p. 21); Chased, Being (p. 48); Lost, Being (p. 155); Paralysis/Running in Slow Motion (p. 178); Swamp (p. 218)

53. **KITCHEN**

Common Manifestations: You are walking through a house in your dream, and you enter the kitchen. It's warm there, and perhaps a pleasant smell hints at a delicious meal being prepared.

Or, the kitchen could be deserted, and you open the cupboards to find them bare and dusty.

The Spin: The house is a very personal, immediate dream symbol, one that can evoke a specific time in someone's life, but can also serve as a metaphor for the self. Particular rooms of a house, and the function of those rooms, often reflect a particular aspect of the dreamer's personality. The kitchen has great emotional resonance as the hub of the modern family household, the place where meals are prepared and often where they are shared. Take a look at the character of your dream kitchen: Was it homey and welcoming, or deserted and austere? This could speak to what your mind is "cooking up" at the moment and whether you're getting the proper emotional nourishment from those around you.

What Freud Would Say: In *The Interpretation of Dreams*, Freud stated, "Rooms in dreams are usually women; if the various ways in and out of them are represented, this interpretation is scarcely open to doubt." Not one to leave any sexual stone unturned, he also argued that a "dream of going through a suite of rooms is a brothel or harem dream." The kitchen, as a stereotypically female room, may have had some significance for Freud.

What Jung Would Say: The house is a metaphor for the Self. Through dreaming, you will learn about aspects of the Self that you have previously repressed or obscured. The kitchen is where one creates and then ingests material, according to the Jungian dream analysis Web site mythsdreamssymbols.com. Kitchen and cooking imagery could allude to your attempt to process sensory input you've received.

Cultural Context:

The kitchen was not always the heart of the family home. In ancient Rome, often lower classes did not even have kitchens in their homes—they traveled to large public kitchens to cook meals. In homes of the upper class, from ancient Rome through the nineteenth century, the kitchen usually was set far apart from the family's living quarters. In earlier times, this had a practical reason, as cooking was done over an open fire that generated considerable smoke. But throughout history, kitchens in wealthy homes were the province of slaves and servants, and as such were separated from the rest of the house.

Related Images:

Attic (p. 24); Basement (p. 26); Corridors/Hallways (p. 64); Home, Childhood (p. 136); Rooms, Secret (p. 199); Rooms, Unused (p. 202)

54. **LIVER**

Common Manifestations:

Although not a common image, some people do dream of eating liver (usually not one's own!) or of having some type of liver ailment.

The Spin:

The liver is the human body's filter and detoxifier, with its primary functions to metabolize carbohydrates, proteins, and fats and remove toxins from the blood (especially alcohol). In this way, a liver dream could be a warning to cut back on your drinking, or it could be a more metaphoric, coded message to remove the people or situations in your life that are poisoning your physical or mental health.

Psychologist and author Gillian Holloway believes that the presence of your liver in a dream is actually a pun, since the word *liver* can also be defined as "one who lives." For Holloway, such a dream is more of a message to take the time to enjoy life and live it up a little.

What Freud Would Say:

Although he did not address dreams of the liver directly, early in *The Interpretation of Dreams*, Freud quoted several of his medical and psychological contemporaries on how dreams can telegraph the presence of internal medical disorders. Freud used this conclusion—what he called the "diagnostic power of dreams"—to make the argument that if physical disease can be expressed in the mysterious language of dreams, then so could psychological disorders. That premise allowed him to pursue the revolutionary path of analyzing a patient's dreams as a means of diagnosing their neuroses.

What Jung Would Say:

In his autobiography, *Memories, Dreams, Reflections*, Jung related a dream he had of visiting a man in

Liverpool, England, in which he stated, "The 'liver,' according to an old view, is the seat of life—that which 'makes to live.'"

Cultural Context:
Interestingly, given the liver's crucial role in protecting the human body, the bile the organ secretes in order to break down fats has traditionally stood for bitterness or ill temper. This association may have something to do with the grisly tale from Greek mythology of Prometheus, the Titan who created humanity. Prometheus stole fire from Mount Olympus to give man an advantage over the beasts. This enraged Zeus, ruler of Olympus, and as punishment, he ordered Prometheus chained to a rock, where an eagle would come, every day, and devour his liver. The liver was regenerated every night so the torture would continue the next day. Eventually, Prometheus was rescued by Hercules.

Related Images:
Mechanical Malfunction (p. 158); Mouth and Teeth (p. 166); Teeth Falling Out (p. 219)

55. **LOST, BEING**

Common Manifestations:
You are in an unfamiliar location—a strange neighborhood or a deserted wilderness. Or perhaps the setting is familiar, but nothing is where you expect it to be. You wander, disoriented, unable to get your

bearings. You might be alone, with no one to ask for help, or the people you encounter might be too intimidating to approach. You grow increasingly frantic with the need to find your way home.

Variations: You ask people for help, but no one seems to understand what you're saying—either you are speaking a different language, or people stubbornly misunderstand your requests (p. 55).

The Spin: This dream is pretty straightforward. You are looking for a sense of direction—either in a career, in a relationship, or simply in your everyday life. Such a dream can also allude to a spiritual crisis. Often, the dream arises at a time when you're having trouble making an important decision—when you, quite literally, don't know which path to take. Try to identify the feelings that arose when you were lost in the dream, and whether those feelings correspond to your reaction to a waking-life situation. Pinpointing when and why you've felt disoriented will make it easier to get yourself on the right path—that is, to decide the course of action that best suits you and your needs.

What Freud   In a similar assessment of falling dreams (p. 107),
Would Say: Freud believed that women often dreamed of different kinds of loss as a metaphor for the anxiety surrounding the loss of virginity or fertility.

What Jung Would Say:	This dream signifies the problems and challenges you face during the search for the Self.
Cultural Context: 📖	Perhaps the most moving and recognized tale of someone trying to find the way home is Homer's epic poem *The Odyssey*, which recounts the trials and missteps of the Greek soldier-king Odysseus (Ulysses) as he sails back to Ithaca after the Trojan War. The gods of Olympus—chiefly, Poseidon, Athena, and Zeus—bicker about his future, and as a consequence Odysseus is frequently thrown off course. The journey is fraught with tests of his bravery, ingenuity, and spirit. He and his men escape from the Lotus-Eaters, who destroy the will to return home. They kill the Cyclops, Polyphemus, and best the twin dangers of the sea-monster Scylla and the whirlpool of Charybdis. Odysseus is imprisoned by the witch-goddess Circe, and then by the nymph Calypso. Finally, twenty years after departing Troy, Odysseus returns to Ithaca, disguised as a beggar, to reclaim his rightful place as king, husband, and father. His loyal wife, Penelope, and son, Telemachus, have steadfastly repelled a gaggle of avaricious suitors as they awaited and hoped for his return.
Related Images:	Communication Breakdown (p. 55); Falling (p. 107); Purse or Wallet, Lost (p. 193)

56.   **MECHANICAL MALFUNCTION**

Common
Manifestations:

Something's not working the way you want it to.
Your car won't start, your computer freezes up, the
iron scorches your favorite shirt, the oven burns
dinner, or maybe the washing machine sprays
water all over the house. You try to fix it, but
either you don't have the know-how, or the problem is deeper than you first realized. Whatever the
scenario, you're rattled and confused by the time
you wake up.

Variations:

A more ominous version of this dream often puts you
behind the wheel of an out-of-control car, where you
are unable to steer, the brakes have failed, or you're
stuck in the path of a large, speeding vehicle and can't
move the car out of the way (p. 41).

The Spin:

Here we see how the machine in your dream could
symbolize an aspect of your life or your personality.
Your computer crashed? Maybe your mind is feeling
blocked by a problem that nags at you. You don't
know how to fix the car? You may feel similarly in over
your head in a waking-life situation. Expect a certain
amount of wish fulfillment as well: If the dishwasher's
on the fritz, then you can't very well do the dishes,
can you? Bummer. If the focus of your dream is an
out-of-control car, then perhaps you're feeling over-
worked and ineffectual, stuck on a path you don't

want to take but unable to steer your life in the direction you want it to go.

Interestingly, some analysts believe that dreams of malfunction may be prodromal, or messages from the unconscious that warn of a looming health crisis. The theory is that your mind may detect physical problems earlier than you realize, and therefore the dream of a broken machine might be connected to some failing with your physical self. If you encounter this dream, it's worth taking a moment to assess the state of your general well-being.

If Recurrent: Make an appointment with a doctor for a full physical.

What Freud Would Say: Not surprisingly, Freud considered cars to be phallic symbols, explaining that dreams of broken-down cars represented fears of impotence.

What Jung Would Say: Trying to pilot an out-of-control car represents the anxiety you feel over trying to take charge of your psychological well-being. Struggling with broken-down machines could be a metaphor for the internal battle you face with negative emotions or unhealthy attitudes.

Cultural Context: Mechanical malfunctions are the stuff of great slapstick comedy—a fixture of the silent comedies of Buster Keaton and a favorite plot point for the classic TV show *I Love Lucy* (who could forget Lucy and Ethel's misadventures as they baked bread and worked a candy-factory assembly line?). In waking life, such missteps are usually a petty inconvenience or fodder for cocktail party anecdotes. Yet interestingly, in the dream world, these scenarios can assume surreal, deeply frustrating, even ominous, overtones.

Related Images: Car Trouble/Driving Problems (p. 41); Communication Breakdown (p. 55); Connections, Missed (p. 61); Paralysis/Running in Slow Motion (p. 178)

---

57. 📷 **MONSTERS**

Common Manifestations: You're face to face with a monster, and it terrifies you. It could be a mythical creature such as a dragon, werewolf, or vampire, but it could be a monster that exists only in the recesses of your own mind. You may be hiding from it, or the monster may be chasing you. It's possible you're fighting the monster in your dream, but the level of fear you're feeling indicates you believe the monster to be invincible.

Variations: A specific version of this dream, which occurs most often in childhood, is to imagine a sinister creature lurks under the bed (p. 31).

Occurrence: Monster dreams are common during adolescence and at times in our adulthood when we don't feel in control of our lives.

The Spin: Most psychoanalysts believe that dream monsters represent particular aspects of your personality that might feel dangerous or compulsive. For teenagers in the throes of puberty, the monster could be their own sexuality. The type of monster in your dream, as well as the monster's salient characteristics, are also relevant. If a werewolf is stalking you, perhaps you feel that someone in your waking life is trying to overpower you or tear your life to shreds. A vampire closing in for the bite could symbolize a person who is leeching off of you like a parasite. If your dream self is grappling with a fire-breathing dragon, you might be on a quest for truth or buried treasure (sometimes those are one and the same). The dragon is what stands between you and whatever you seek, and slaying the dragon usually means you have conquered your fears and are ready to wield your true power. It's interesting to note that in cultural traditions of Asia, dragons are not evil, but a source of wisdom.

If Recurrent: Stop watching those creature features before bedtime. And stock up on holy water.

What Freud Would Say: Monsters or other beasts that appear in dreams usually represent repressed urges that scare or intimidate the dreamer. Freud speculated, not surprisingly, that the beast symbolized sexual aggression and power (even more so if the beast is hiding under the bed). He also believed that the dreamer turned this repressed urge into an entirely different creature in order to disassociate from it and alleviate the anxiety that such feelings cause.

What Jung Would Say:

Worrying about monsters under the bed is a likely indication that something powerful in your unconscious is pushing its way to the surface, demanding to be reckoned with. One of the foundations of Jung's world of mystical symbolism and the collective unconscious is the notion of the hero's journey; in this case, the hero must identify and conquer his inner demons in order to progress toward self-knowledge or individuation.

Cultural Context:

The equation of monsters with sexuality and teenage rites of passage has spawned countless schlocky horror flicks (remember, the promiscuous kids were always the first ones killed in the *Friday the 13th* movies) and the occasional insightful drama. The long-running cult TV show *Buffy the Vampire Slayer* excelled at portraying high school as a figurative and literal hell. Every week, the title character—the "one girl in all the world with the strength and skill to hunt the vampires, and face the forces of darkness"—battled graveyard-dwelling nasties with a quip and a stake through the heart. But saving the world—a lot—was a piece of cake when compared with the personal battles she waged: with losing her mother, with assuming adult responsibilities, and with resisting the lure of the destructive, bad-boy relationship.

Related Images: Aliens (p. 13); Animal, Attack by Wild (p. 17);
                  Animals (p. 21); Chased, Being (p. 48);
                  Paralysis/Running in Slow Motion (p. 178)

58.   **MOTHER**

Common   It's all Mom, all the time. Mom gets top billing in
Manifestations: your dream, which might be enough to irk you right
                off the bat. Perhaps you are dreaming of a new
                encounter, in which you say nice, soft things you've
                never had the chance to say to each other. Or you
                may be living out a scene, positive or negative, played
                in waking life hundreds of times—you and your mom
                laughing over dinner, lounging around your parents'
                home, or arguing bitterly over a choice you have made.

Variations: You might also dream of your mother's death, though
                she is still alive in real life (p. 73). Or you may dream
                you are having sex with your mother (p. 211).

The Spin: It's easy to claim that the family matriarch symbolizes
    ???   a need for comfort and security—this is true, to a cer-
                tain extent, but rarely are family relationships so uni-
                lateral. Parents are only human, after all, and they
                come with their own emotional baggage to contend
                with. To decode what your dream mother is trying to
                tell you, you need to pay attention to the dream's setting,
                time, and background characters. How old are you in

the dream? At that age, how did you feel about your mom—was she The One Who Kisses Away the Pain, or The Thorn in Your Side? Where did the dream take place, and what associations do you have with that setting? Your mind chose to take you back to this particular period for a reason—most likely to shed light on a situation or problem you're currently facing. Understanding the connection between your dream past and your waking present could highlight unhealthy behavior patterns, and with time and insight, history will cease to repeat itself.

Dreams of death are primarily signifiers of transformation and transition—of turning over a new leaf or moving on to a new phase of your life. Adolescents often dream of one or both of their parents dying in a metaphoric expression of their growing independence. Dreams of having sex with your mother are unlikely to be a symptom of repressed childhood abuse. Instead, the connection your unconscious is making may be more complex and metaphorical. Your current partner might simply share a significant personality trait with your mother, and in real life you find yourself responding to him or her with the same old behavior patterns.

What Freud Would Say:

One could argue that Freud's bread and butter, the central hypotheses of his psychoanalytic theory, were the Oedipus and Electra complexes—that men unconsciously want to kill their fathers and have sex with their mothers, and that women want to kill their mothers and have sex with their fathers, and that both men and women spend a great deal of psychic energy repressing that realization. Freud believed that young boys and girls viewed their same-sex parent as a rival for the other parent's affection, and that it's not a stretch to imagine an impulsive, id-governed child wishing for a parent's death. Regarding mothers and daughters specifically, Freud stated, "Occasions for conflict between a daughter and her mother arise when the daughter begins to grow up and long for sexual liberty, but finds herself under her mother's tutelage; while the mother, on the other hand, is warned by her daughter's growth that the time has come when she herself must abandon her claims to sexual satisfaction."

What Jung Would Say:	Among Jung's many archetypes of the collective unconscious was that of the Great Mother, symbol of all things feminine and the embodiment of the life and death cycles in nature. The Great Mother is also a symbol of the unconscious (as contrasted with the Spiritual Father, a symbol of consciousness), and as such, has the ability to enrich life through self-knowledge and enlightenment or to destroy life through psychosis.
Related Images:	Death of Loved One (Unrelated to Actual Death) (p. 73); Deceased Loved One, Visit from (p. 79); Father (p. 109); Sex with Someone You Know (Not Your Partner) (p. 211)

59.   **MOUTH AND TEETH**

Common
Manifestations:

You are going about your everyday business when you suddenly taste blood in your mouth. A tooth has come loose, and as you reach up to your lips, it falls out, and you spit it into your hand. Alarmed, you soon feel one tooth after the other separating from your gums, as you struggle to staunch the blood and save the teeth. Another take on the losing-your-teeth dream is where your teeth crumble out of your open mouth like broken cookies.

Variations:

Your teeth, instead of falling out, are growing into fangs or becoming so gnarled that you can't speak or ingest food. Perhaps you're trying to eat a meal, but everything you put into your mouth is tasteless—or you might be able to taste the food, but you chew endlessly, without swallowing.

Occurrence:

The dream of losing your teeth is likely to occur during middle age, at times of great responsibility, and perhaps as you enter senior citizenship.

The Spin:

Teeth are a fundamental symbol of self and a barometer of both physical and psychological well-being. According to psychologist and author Gillian Holloway, when you dream that your teeth are diseased or misshapen, it's probably a sign that you're not being true to yourself, or that you're in a work or personal situation that is a bad fit. Teeth are also instruments of biting, chewing, and eating, and as such can be considered both symbols of aggression as well as concrete representations of how we "digest" the stimuli all around us. In that respect, a dream of endlessly chewing food could indicate an indecisive nature—you contemplate and "chew on" issues without moving on to actually make a decision.

???

Dreams of losing your teeth are surprisingly common and have little to do with dental phobia. In this case, your teeth are a metaphoric signpost for times of great life change. Baby teeth fall out as you enter adolescence, and wisdom teeth come in as you become an adult. The onset of old age goes hand in hand with the deterioration of your teeth. So losing your teeth can be understood as an expression of insecurity at the prospect of upcoming change. The shame and embarrassment associated with the loss of your teeth can also parallel feelings of inadequacy or lack of confidence during times of stress.

If Recurrent: Fight those cavities, and don't forget to floss.

What Freud Dreams "with a dental stimulus" reflect a desire for
Would Say: masturbation in both men and women. Additionally, for men, the missing-teeth dream expresses a fear of castration. Although the connection between the penis and teeth may seem entirely arbitrary, Freud believed that sexual repression in the dreamer caused

a "transposition" of the penis anxiety (in the lower part of the body) into dental anxiety (in the upper part of the body). Freud also believed that, for women, the dream of losing teeth symbolized a desire to have children.

What Jung Would Say:
A dream of losing your teeth indicates that you are anxious about losing power and vitality as you age.

Cultural Context:
According to Gayle Delaney, author of *In Your Dreams*, the losing-your-teeth dream casts a long shadow throughout history. First mention can be traced all the way back to the Chester Beatty papyrus, an ancient Egyptian dream manual dating from 2000 BCE. Here, the loss of one's teeth augurs the dreamer's murder by his family. The Talmud records a similar prophecy: Dream of losing your teeth, and expect a death in the family. In 200 CE, the Greek scholar Artemidorus—perhaps the world's first dream expert—wrote a book that examined the dream interpretation traditions of ancient Greece and Rome. In it, he presents teeth as a metaphor for social standing. If you dream of losing your teeth, he claims, you will lose power and possessions. But conversely, if a slave dreams of losing his teeth, he will soon win his freedom.

Related Images:
Lost, Being (p. 155); Purse or Wallet, Lost (p. 193); Teeth Falling Out (p. 219)

60.   **MUD**

Common
Manifestations:

Talk about your messy dreams. In this one, you're dirty, and you're stuck. Mud is all around you—perhaps you are on foot or in a vehicle. But the thick, viscous matter has you bogged down, and you can't go anywhere. The more you struggle to escape, the filthier and more entrenched you become.

Variations:

Dreams of quicksand follow a similar pattern, as do dreams of being stuck in a mucky swamp. Rarely are mud dreams positive, with the possible exception of (purposefully) taking a mud bath as a spa treatment.

The Spin:

Mud represents a blending of earth (terra firma, the things we know empirically) and water (the mysterious depths, the unconscious). So the appearance of mud in a dream in which you feel "stuck" is a wonderfully evocative metaphor for a conflict between logic and emotion, between the head and the heart. Quicksand has much the same quality, with an added twist of surprise: Those quicksand pits appear out of nowhere, when you least expect it. But focusing only on the conflict prevents any attempt to address the heart of the problem.

Mud obviously carries negative personal connotations as well. Who hasn't been the victim of mudslinging, or had one's name dragged through the mud? This might be the unconscious commenting obliquely on how you're perceived at the moment.

Have you undertaken a relationship or endeavor that has "sullied" your good name or reputation? Is a love or family relationship dragging you down, keeping you from making progress?

If Recurrent: Invest in a good detergent, or at the very least, some enzyme-based stain remover.

What Freud Would Say: Mud and dirt are classic Freudian substitutes for feces. Dreams that evoke anal imagery likely address unresolved feelings of shame, resentment, and often monetary greed. Freud made this psychic connection through one of his customary reversals: Feces are something toxic released from the body, and these unconscious urges toward greed, anger, and shame involve holding on to something or keeping negative feelings hidden from others.

What Jung Would Say: Jung did not specifically address dreams of mud, but he did talk at length about humankind's "earthly" nature, the connection we all have to the earth: "That we are bound to the earth does not mean we cannot grow. . . . No noble, well-grown tree ever disowned its dark roots, for it grows not only upward, but downward as well." Jung also equated "mother" earth with a type of feminine life force (the archetype of the Anima) and the unconscious: Being connected with this part of yourself allows you to progress along the path of individuation.

Cultural
Context:

Jung's notion of the earth as a primal feminine life force can be traced to creation myths involving humanity being sculpted out of or emerging from the mud. There is, of course, the story in the Old Testament book of Genesis that God made man in his own image, breathing life into a handful of dirt. The Navajo people passed along stories of a powerful being called Changing Woman, who, along with her husband, the Sun, and their twin sons, saved this world from monsters that sought to kill the Earth People. According to the legend, Changing Woman made her own people to keep her company during the day, as her husband was traveling across the sky. They were known as the Mud People, Salt Water People, Near Water People, and Bitter Water People. In China, a deity called Nu Gua created two classes of people; she shaped yellow clay into human forms, and breathed life into them.

And finally, sacred texts of the Quiche Maya of Guatemala refer to gods who wanted to create beings who would worship them. In their first attempt, they sculpted beings out of mud, but these Mud People disintegrated every time it rained, so the gods grew impatient with the imperfection of the Mud People and abandoned them. Some scholars believe that, in light of the Maya's political and religious conquest by European soldiers, this story is intended to mock the Christian creation story. The Maya distrusted and despised their ruthless, brutal conquerors, and in adopting this tale, they perhaps sought to underscore the irony of a people believing they had been fashioned from the earth, when those same people were intent on systematically exploiting and depleting Earth's resources.

Related Images: Elimination, Inappropriate or Inconvenient (p. 94); Paralysis/Running in Slow Motion (p. 178); Rain (p. 194)

---

61. **NATURAL DISASTERS: EARTHQUAKES, HURRICANES, TORNADOES, AND VOLCANOES**

Common Manifestations: This is a terrifying dream. Something earth-shaking (often literally) is taking place. You may be experiencing the trauma firsthand, or you may be watching it from afar as it affects others, with no ability to prevent the destruction. The powerlessness you feel both during and after the catastrophe is potent and frustrating.

Variations: This type of dream could also encompass dreams of dangerous water (p. 230) or storms (p. 194).

Occurrence: This dream is common among people who have difficulty expressing emotion. People who live in areas prone to natural disasters may simply dream of reliving the horror, or may be expressing anxiety about the possibility of a disaster.

The Spin: As obvious metaphors go, disaster dreams are not exactly the type you can, or should, ignore. Either you've finally connected to your inner exaggerator ("I'm buried under an avalanche of paperwork! I'm going to blow my top if you don't leave me alone!"), or you've been ignoring a real-life emotional crisis at your own risk. Leaving legitimate global warming premonitions aside, natural disaster dreams are a smack-you-over-the-head warning that your inner life is not as stable as it should be. And the type of disaster your mind chooses for its dream script can be telling as well.

According to Jungian dream analyst Jeremy Taylor, tornadoes have long been called "the finger of God," and indeed often represent sudden, awesome change that hints at a profound spiritual transformation. Dream dictionary author Sandra Thomson believes that earthquake dreams signify a "breakthrough"—something vital is trying to break through from the unconscious to the conscious mind. Volcano dreams, not surprisingly, are unsubtle attempts to address powerful emotions you're having a hard time keeping under control. Life-threatening water dreams are signs that your waking-life emotions are volatile and potentially overwhelming. The sensation of struggling against—and being defeated by—a powerful force of nature is an apt metaphor for how overwhelmed you can feel by your emotions, or by a seemingly intractable situation. Think about how a tsunami, associated with the unforgiving ocean and underwater earthquakes, could sweep you away suddenly, without warning. Or how rising flood waters could inexorably swallow you, despite your attempts to control the overflow.

The good news is that dreaming of the natural disaster—that is, envisioning the nightmare scenario coming true—is, in a way, a vote of confidence in your ability to weather the emotional storm. Simply having the dream indicates that your unconscious is working over the issue and trying to help you deal with it. The implication is that once the worst has passed, a fresh outlook settles over that which was destroyed. The same holds true for the natural world: Volcanoes spew lava and ash, which fertilizes the soil. Earthquakes are necessary to keep the earth stable—maybe your foundations have been shaken to their core recently?

What Freud Would Say:

It's not a stretch to say that Freud would assign a sexual or ejaculatory meaning to any dream of an active volcano. He also argued that dreams in which the water, in whatever form, turned sinister could indicate anxiety about sex and repression of forbidden thoughts of bed-wetting.

What Jung Would Say:

Dream earthquakes are signs that your life could be falling apart, and that your emotional stability is on perilous ground. Water is often representative of feminine energy (the Anima) and symbolizes the mystery of the unconscious. Large bodies of water such as the oceans and seas are archetypal symbols for the collective unconscious. Men who fear water in real life may harbor fears of women or of their emotional/feminine side.

Related Images: Drowning/Breathing Underwater (p. 84); Mud (p. 169); Paralysis/Running in Slow Motion (p. 178); Rain (p. 194); Water (p. 230)

62. **NUDITY, PUBLIC**

Common Manifestations: You are in a public place—at school, a party, or in your office—and suddenly realize you are without clothes. Perhaps you're only partially naked—no pants, or maybe your undergarments do not sufficiently cover the important bits. Mortified, you try desperately to hide or to find something to cover yourself. However, no one seems to notice your absence of clothes.

Variations: You are in a public place but are not embarrassed by your nakedness. Or you and the characters in your dream are both scandalized by your nakedness.

Occurrence: This dream usually first occurs during adolescence. During adulthood, it may reoccur during times of great change, insecurity, or waning self-confidence.

The Spin:

???

In times of crisis, nudity dreams signify the adoption of a new identity. Recently, something good has happened to you—a promotion, a new romance, public notoriety—and you're uneasy about the change, unconfident of your ability to meet this new responsibility, or uncomfortable with the increased attention. You feel your shortcomings will be "exposed." However, if in the dream no one else notices your nakedness, this usually indicates that the insecurity is entirely self-generated. If your customary skills or defenses (your metaphysical "clothes") are not sufficient for this new role, you will develop an entirely new "wardrobe" for the situation. If, in the dream, you are unashamed that you're naked, this could mean you are comfortable being yourself or that you are shedding an old role for a new one.

If the people in your dream are outraged by your nakedness, then perhaps you have offended someone in your waking life by giving voice to censored or inappropriate thoughts. And according to nineteenth-century dream analyst Gustavus Hindman Miller, to dream that you suddenly discover your nudity and are trying to conceal it means you have "sought illicit pleasure contrary to your noblest instincts and are desirous of abandoning those desires." If a young woman dreams of swimming naked in clear water, she will "enjoy illicit loves, but nature will revenge her by sickness, or loss of charms."

What Freud Would Say:	You are daring to expose yourself. You have an infantile desire to break rules and regain the childhood freedom of exhibiting your naked body without shame.
What Jung Would Say:	Clothing is a metaphor for the Persona, or the self you present to the outside world. When you find yourself naked in a dream, it means that in your waking life, you have revealed more of your authentic self than is socially acceptable. This kind of dream allows you to explore the difference between your inner self and outer self.
Cultural Context:	Nakedness in public, and the shame associated with it, has historically reflected each culture's notion of what is morally or socially acceptable. In many tropical, desert, or island societies, toplessness or seminudity has practical, not prurient, implications. Keeping cool under the harsh sun is the priority, and for many African and Indonesian cultures, toplessness does not provoke the same scandalized or titillated reaction it does in some predominantly white, Western cultures. In the Northern and Western European tradition— where colder climates necessitate wearing more clothes for protection from the elements—public nudity is discouraged, and those who flaunt these conventions are treated as pariahs. In one notorious (though likely apocryphal) instance dating back to the eleventh century, long-haired Lady Godiva, the much younger wife of Leofric, Earl of Mercia, rode naked

on horseback down the main street in her hometown of Coventry, England. She did so on a dare from her husband, and in return he agreed to lessen the tax burden on the local peasants.

Related Images: Elimination, Inappropriate or Inconvenient (p. 94); Exam/Public Performance (p. 101); Sex in Public (p. 208)

63.   **PARALYSIS/RUNNING IN SLOW MOTION**

Common Manifestations: In the dream, you are trying to escape from a threat, someone who conveys danger to you. But as you run away, your legs move with agonizing slowness. Either you have little to no muscle control (meaning no matter how badly you want to leave, your legs won't do what you tell them to do), or the effort is simply too great—it feels as if you're moving through quicksand. You realize, with consternation, that the person is gaining on you, and you just can't move any faster. Most people wake up, panicked, before getting captured.

Variations: It's not always a person you're unsuccessfully trying to evade—frequent dreams of this type also involve trying to avoid being hit by a car or a train or trying to outrun a tidal wave, tornado, avalanche, or other immutable force of nature.

Occurrence: This dream often crops up at a time when you have to make an important decision.

The Spin: We're talking inner conflict, pure and simple. You're
??? 👊 feeling "stuck" in a life situation and struggling to find a way out. Or perhaps the situation is more passive, and you're trapped by choice: A big decision looms on the horizon—breaking off a relationship, changing careers, starting a family, selling a house—and you're afraid to take that step forward. In either case, your mind unconsciously associates some danger with moving on, with making progress. That you struggle against your paralysis in the dream indicates that at least part of you wants to make that leap forward. To help understand where and why your dream self is paralyzed, break down how you react in the dream when you can't run away (panicked, angry, frustrated, hopeless), and whether that corresponds to your feelings about a real-life challenge you face. By understanding the source of your dream anxiety and inertia, you might gain a new perspective on your waking life and find the motivation you need to make a change.

What Freud As with dreams of being chased, Freud felt that dream-
Would Say: ing of an inability to run indicated that the dreamer wanted to be caught. Not surprisingly, Freud believed this unconscious desire had a sexual connotation; the dream represented a wish to be caught and ravished.

What Jung Would Say:	Jung believed that dreams provided a window into the mysteries of the psyche and afforded great opportunity for self-knowledge. For him, the characters in a dream usually represented aspects of one's own personality. So, in struggling to escape someone or something, you are actually failing to acknowledge or reconcile an important, but perhaps intimidating, part of yourself. The inability to effectively escape within the dream indicates the inevitability of addressing these issues.
Biological Context:	Although the paralysis felt in this dream often points to unresolved emotional issues, scientists believe there also may be an underlying physical cause: sleep paralysis. When the body descends into REM sleep—the stage when dreaming is most likely—the brain initiates partial or complete muscular paralysis to prevent the body from reacting physically to a dream scenario. Occasionally, when a person wakes from REM sleep, the paralysis persists for several moments longer and is sometimes accompanied by vivid hallucinations—a potentially terrifying one-two punch.
Related Images:	Animal, Attack by Wild (p. 17); Chased, Being (p. 48); Crime, Victim of (p. 70); Monsters (p. 160); Mud (p. 169)

64. **PARTNER/SPOUSE**

Common
Manifestations:

Your significant other plays a starring role in this dream, be it a comedy, romance, or drama. Perhaps you're making happy memories—traveling somewhere peaceful or exotic, having a baby, moving into a new house. Overcome with passion, you may search madly for a place to have sex (p. 206) or perhaps throw caution to the wind and make love in public (p. 208). On the down side, you could be bickering over a long-standing issue—even one as inane as taking out the garbage—or, in a crushing blow, discovering your partner's infidelity (p. 142).

Variations:

A single person might occasionally dream of being married, even if he or she isn't currently attached.

The Spin:

Dreams about your spouse or partner are intensely personal, reflective of not just your relationship, but how you see yourself within the context of that relationship. Happy dreams of couplehood serve to reinforce the bond between you. If your dream presents barriers to intimacy—someone watching you have sex, interruptions during private moments—you may feel scrutinized or self-conscious in the relationship, or wonder if people or life circumstances are conspiring to sabotage a good thing in your life. Dream dictionary author Sandra Thomson believes that dreaming you are attached or married when you are avowedly single could hint at an unacknowledged need for security and nurturing.

 Dreams of marital strife, no matter how inane, can be highly unsettling, but could speak to areas of the relationship that are dissatisfying or unfulfilling. Picturing your partner as unfaithful, however, doesn't have to be taken literally. Do you have legitimate waking-life suspicions? Or are you just anxious at the thought of losing a stable, happy relationship?

What Freud Would Say: Freud believed that dreams often distorted the secret wishes that the unconscious intended them to express. So in discussing the dream with a patient, he often conducted what he called reversals—understanding a dream symbol as the embodiment of its opposite. In this way, for Freud, dreaming of a partner's infidelity could indicate your unconscious desire to have an adulterous relationship yourself. The principle of wish fulfillment would also imply that dreaming of being interrupted during sex implies your unconscious desire to be observed having sex—or, to have sex with the person who interrupts you.

What Jung Would Say: For Jung, sex symbolized a union of the masculine and feminine energies in each person's nature; it is this synthesis and balance of opposing forces that account for developmental progression. "Masculine" energy in women is defined by the Animus, which signifies action, analytic ability, and conviction.

Archetypal manifestations of the Animus include the Spiritual Father and the Wise Old Man (a mentor, priest, or respected elder). Similarly, "feminine" energy in men is symbolized by the Anima, which encompasses intuition, introspection, and emotion. The primary archetypal example of the Anima is the Great Mother, an earthy, fertile Mother Nature–type figure who embodies the mysteries of the unconscious mind.

Related Images:

Father (p. 109); Infidelity (p. 142); Mother (p. 163); Sex, Interrupted/Nowhere to Make Love (p. 206); Sex in Public (p. 208); Sex with Someone You Know (Not Your Partner) (p. 211)

65. 📷

POLICE OFFICERS

Common Manifestations:

The cops are on to you. You've been pulled over on the highway, hailed while you're walking down the sidewalk, or pulled out of your office for an interrogation. You're forced to answer to your whereabouts and your actions. You might even get roughed up in the process. Usually, this dream evokes fear—of being arrested or imprisoned—but occasionally you'll feel only defiance in the face of condemnation and suspicion.

Variations:

The officer may not just stop at chitchat; you may be arrested for committing a crime (p. 66) or even sent to jail (p. 190).

Occurrence: This is a common dream during adolescence and puberty, when your reflexive tendency is to chafe against any restrictions on your behavior.

The Spin: Images of police officers are fairly straightforward representations of authority figures, a category that encompasses parents (usually fathers) as well as your own internal censors. So dreams of this nature can be interpreted as snapshots of your psychic relationship with authority—whether that authority is imposed from within or without.

Dreams that focus on capture and punishment express feelings of guilt, either for actions you have taken in waking life or for self-destructive or negative feelings you have harbored. (Often, you are your own harshest judge.) Do you recognize the identity of the officer in the dream, or does the person symbolize a larger issue or idea? How did you respond to the officer? Were you contrite and cooperative— implying that you respect the officer's authority— or did you resist arrest? Defying the authority in your dream could be perceived as a way to regain power in your waking life. The nuance of this dream is also influenced by your relationship with the police in waking life; do you trust law enforcement implicitly, or have you been the victim of unjustified harassment?

If Recurrent:	If you work in the law enforcement industry, these dreams could simply be rehearsals that ready you for another day on the job.
What Freud Would Say:	In *The Interpretation of Dreams*, Freud related the story of a friend who dreamt he was standing outside his home with a woman when the police arrived and arrested him for infanticide. Freud discovered that the man had been conducting a secret affair with a married woman, practicing birth control to avoid an unwanted pregnancy. Freud deduced that the man felt guilt over the desire to avoid a pregnancy, and that therefore the dream arrest was the fulfillment of the man's wish to be punished. The actions of the police officer could easily be interpreted as coming directly from the man's superego.
What Jung Would Say:	For Jung, the dream character that interrogates you could represent the Shadow archetype, which symbolizes the "dark" and creative part of the personality. With this darkness comes a wellspring of untapped potential, and Jung believed that no true spiritual or psychological growth could take place without reconciliation with the Shadow—setting the Shadow free, as it were. Alternatively, in a woman's dream, the officer could represent the Animus archetype, that is, the masculine life principle that is often associated with analysis and judgment.

Cultural
Context:

To paint in broad strokes, organized society operates under the collective assumption that those we invest with authority wield it appropriately. Feeling wrongly pursued or accused by those who are trusted to "protect and serve" can evoke the kind of creeping dread that makes for a great existential novel—namely, Franz Kafka's 1925 work *The Trial* (in German, *Der Prozess*). In it, an unassuming bank drone, Joseph K., is one day arrested for a crime that is never specified. The unrelentingly grim novel recounts Joseph's attempts to navigate the dadaist legal system, though to call it a system implies a level of recognizable order missing from the tale—one reason the book is most often described as "nightmarish." Joseph is unable to mount a defense, unable even to understand the progression of his fate. In the end, he almost welcomes his brutal murder as his only avenue for escape.

Alfred Hitchcock's films often similarly portray police officers as menacing custodians of unchecked authority—in *Psycho*, the audience shares Marion Crane's dread of an officer wearing reflective sunglasses that mask his eyes and his emotions.

Related Images:

Chased, Being (p. 48); Crime, Committing (p. 66); Crime, Victim of (p. 70); Prison (p. 190)

66. PREGNANCY/GIVING BIRTH

Common
Manifestations:

You are pregnant and about to become a parent, though you may or may not be expecting in waking life. Often the dream pregnancy has unusual characteristics; it could last an exceptionally short or long term, or perhaps you aren't gestating a human baby. Many dreamers carry the scenario through labor and delivery, with the attendant stress, discomfort, and euphoria. Interestingly, this dream isn't just for women—men report vivid pregnancy dreams as well.

Variations:

Pregnant women dream throughout the gestational period. According to Sandra Thomson, author of *Cloud Nine: A Dreamer's Dictionary*, common dreams during this period include growing flowers or fruit, recollections of one's own mother, and nightmares of giving birth to a deformed or sick child.

Occurrence:

This dream often arises during parenting years, or during times of great change in your career or personal life.

The Spin:

If you're not pregnant in real life, the symbolism of a birth dream is still quite clear. You have undertaken something that requires a great deal of hard work ("labor") and commitment. Perhaps you have changed careers, started a new venture, or dedicated yourself to a spiritual path. (Don't be surprised if, as a new business owner, you actually "give birth" to your new product.) Expectant fathers often dream not only that they are carrying the child, but going through full labor and delivery as well.

If you are pregnant in waking life, your dreams serve to confront your worries and prepare you for the birth experience. Nightmares of having a damaged baby are less prophetic than instructive. Your subconscious uses the dream world to present you with stressful hypotheticals so you can develop effective coping mechanisms for real life. Some studies have indicated that women who rehearse the birth process in their dreams often have shorter, less stressful deliveries.

If Recurrent:	If you aren't pregnant, you might be having trouble effecting change in your life. If you are pregnant, you can expect recurring dreams throughout your pregnancy.
What Freud Would Say:	Freud believed that people did not dream of birth per se, but that other dream symbols expressed a hidden desire to give birth—among them, images of subterranean canals (p. 43), dark water (p. 230), and even teeth falling out (p. 219), an image in which a part is separated from the whole.
What Jung Would Say:	For Jung, the birth image was a metaphor hinting at new aspects of a personality—a sign of greater self-awareness. Dreams of rebirth are archetypal and call to mind the central tenets of Christian philosophy.

Cultural
Context:

A human pregnancy lasts approximately 266 days, just less than nine months. The mammal that most closely corresponds to this is the cow, with a gestation period of about 284 days. According to the *Guinness Book of World Records*, the Asiatic elephant has the longest pregnancy of any mammal, at an average of 650 days, or more than twenty-one months. The American opossum has the shortest, at an average of only twelve days.

Stories of birth that deviate from the norm are found throughout literature and religion. In Greek mythology, Athena, goddess of knowledge, sprung fully formed (and fully armed) from the forehead of Zeus. Aphrodite, goddess of love, rose out of the seafoam (illustrated beautifully in the Botticelli painting *The Birth of Venus*). Legend states the emperor Julius Caesar was cut from his mother's womb upon birth—hence the term *caesarean section*—although other sources claim his mother, Aurelia, lived well into his twenties, which would make such a procedure unlikely, given medical sophistication at the time. And in the Old Testament book of Genesis, an angel visits the childless couple of Sarah and Abraham to deliver the message that they would soon bear a child. Though Abraham was one hundred years old and Sarah ninety, they were graced with a son, Isaac.

Related Images: Beach/Ocean (p. 28); Child, Forgetting or Misplacing (p. 51)

67. **PRISON**

Common
Manifestations:

You're going to the big house. Perhaps your dream recounts in great detail your crime, trial, and subsequent sentencing, or the dream curtain rises with you already behind bars. You might have no idea why you've been incarcerated. Regardless, you're in jail, and your feelings of despair indicate that you're not getting out any time soon.

The Spin:
???

Dreams that focus on capture and punishment can serve as an expression of guilt—either for actions you have taken in waking life or for negative or self-destructive feelings you have harbored. If the dream zeros in on the particulars of your incarceration, perhaps someone or something is trying to control your behavior or curtail your freedom. Do you chafe against a relationship commitment (being shackled to the "old ball and chain")? Or are you trapped in a job that rewards blind obedience and dronelike behavior? Try to pinpoint the identity of your jailer in the dream: Is it someone you recognize? Or does the person symbolize a larger issue or idea? Is your dream prison imposed from without, in the rules and demands others place on you? Or is it a prison you have built for yourself, with inhibitions and fear keeping you locked away from your heart's desire? Identifying what holds you back as well as who you blame, deep down, for these restrictions will help you address the issue head-on and may dissolve any lingering resentments.

If Recurrent: If you work in the corrections industry, these dreams could simply be a ho-hum rehash of another day at the office.

What Freud Would Say: Freud did not analyze dreams of prisons per se. But in *The Interpretation of Dreams*, he did speculate on the connection between waking-life feelings of guilt and dreams of punishment. He recounted the story of a friend who dreamt he was standing outside his home with a woman when the police arrived and arrested him for infanticide. Freud discovered that the man had been conducting a secret affair with a married woman, practicing birth control to avoid an unwanted pregnancy. Freud deduced that the man felt guilt over the desire to avoid a pregnancy, and that therefore the dream arrest was the fulfillment of the man's wish to be punished.

What Jung Would Say: For Jung, the dream character that imprisons you could represent the Shadow archetype, which symbolizes the "dark" and creative part of the personality. With this darkness comes a wellspring of untapped potential, and Jung believed that no true spiritual or psychological growth could take place without reconciliation with the Shadow—setting the Shadow free, as it were.

Cultural Context:

Sociologists have long believed that the goals of prisons in organized societies should be deterrence (the specter of serving time preventing others from committing crimes), punishment (exacting a price of time and freedom from prisoners for committing a crime), and rehabilitation (working with prisoners to make life on the outside productive and crime-free).

The notion of rehabilitation is an interesting one when applied to your dream scenario—learning about the waking-life situations that make you feel trapped could help you decode your dreams more effectively and perhaps leave your psychic prison behind once and for all. In the real world, incarceration rates are on the rise in the United States despite declining crime rates, owing in large part to harsher sentencing laws. (With more than two million inmates, the United States has the largest prison population in the world, although it ranks only fourth in the world for population.) Increased crowding in prisons, as well as continued privatization of the corrections industry, has meant the large-scale abandonment of rehabilitation and resocialization of the prison population—a decision that, ironically, increases the rate of recidivism and, in turn, the prison population.

Related Images:

Crime, Committing (p. 66); Desert Island (p. 81); Police Officers (p. 183)

68. 📷 **PURSE OR WALLET, LOST**

Common Manifestations:	The setting could be one of many, but the salient characteristic of this dream is that wherever you are, you suddenly realize that you have lost your purse or wallet. Maybe you misplaced it, or someone stole it from you. But rather than feel inconvenienced, you descend quickly into panic.
Occurrence: 👤👥	This dream is common among people who have entered a new phase in their lives—freshman-year college students, new parents, first-time empty nesters, or retirees, for example.
The Spin: ???	A classic anxiety dream. That you are so distraught over a relatively pedestrian crisis implies that the dream is less about a financial hardship and more about how you respond to and process change. Here, the purse or wallet is a tangible representation of your identity. If a recent event has catapulted your life into flux—perhaps a spouse has passed away, or you have moved to a new town—you may feel adrift, and your identity as a wife, husband, parent, student, or professional may seem challenged.
If Recurrent:	Get a copy of your credit report ASAP.
What Freud Would Say:	The purse symbolizes the female womb, and both purses and wallets often represent the vagina. Dreams

of losing your wallet or purse are clear expressions of sexual anxiety. For men, it symbolizes a loss of virility.

What Jung
Would Say:

The wallet is a metaphor for the Persona, and you are worried about a loss of identity and power.

Related Images:

Exam/Public Performance (p. 101); Nudity, Public (p. 175); Teeth Falling Out (p. 219)

---

69. **RAIN**

Common
Manifestations:

It's raining. In the dream, you might be outside, enjoying the day, when you're suddenly caught in a shower. It could be a light mist or a full-on thunder and lightning storm. The dream might also focus on trying to find shelter from the downpour. Rarely is a dream about rain specifically: Usually the rain serves more as a backdrop to the dream scene, setting a mood and lending the dream more emotional nuance.

The Spin:

Rain bears a certain metaphoric resemblance to tears, so it's likely that a rainy dream carries the quality of sadness. It sets the scene for the main plot of the dream ("rain on your parade"), and hints at the underlying emotion. How bad is it: a soft drizzle or a torrential deluge? Try to pinpoint your reaction. Are you alarmed by the intensity of the cloudburst? If so, perhaps someone surprised you—or you surprised yourself—with a vehement outburst you weren't expecting. Or, maybe you welcomed the (emotionally) cleansing rain after a long "dry spell." It allows you to wipe the slate clean and start anew.

A powerful storm is a dream image that conveys two essential messages. On one hand, the tempest might represent your struggle with unexpressed feelings and fears, as you are buffeted by overwhelming emotion. But another, hopeful message is embedded within—no matter how bad the storm is in the moment, it always blows over, restoring calm in its wake. In this way, rain has a natural and healthy role in the life cycle—it clears the air, hydrates animal life, and facilitates seed dispersal and plant reproduction.

If Recurrent:	You might need to give yourself, or someone close to you, the space and the freedom to be sad or mourn, in order to work through some powerful issues.
What Freud Would Say:	Although Freud did not address rain as a meaningful dream symbol, he did argue that water images evoked memories of the womb and birth and regressive thoughts of childhood. Dreams where water, in whatever form, turned sinister could indicate anxiety about sex and repression of forbidden thoughts of bed-wetting.
What Jung Would Say:	Water is often representative of feminine energy (the Anima), and it symbolizes the mystery of the uncon-

scious. Clues in the dream about the nature of the water—clear, polluted, still, or roiling—can speak to the state of the psyche.

Cultural Context:

In the dream universe, rain usually serves a cleansing function. In the material world, rain claims a natural, healthy role in the life cycle—it clears the air, hydrates animal life, and facilitates seed dispersal and plant reproduction. Agrarian societies throughout history have enjoyed bounty or suffered hardship depending on the level of rainfall. In ancient Egyptian, Mayan, Sioux, and Hopi cultures, rain dances were common in times of drought as a way to implore the gods to increase precipitation. Such dances resembled fertility rites; commonly, young girls would dance in a circle to rhythmic percussion as others brandished snakes, long staffs, or other phallic imagery. A modern-day manifestation is the Romanian rite of *paparuda*, a spring ceremony in which a young girl, wearing a dress woven with vines and small branches, travels through her village, stopping at every house so housewives can pour water on her.

Related Images:

Beach/Ocean (p. 28); Natural Disasters: Earthquakes, Hurricanes, Tornadoes, and Volcanoes (p. 172); Water (p. 230)

70. 📷 **RIVERS**

Common
Manifestations:

You are floating down a river in some sort of raft or boat. You could have a destination in mind, or you are simply enjoying the trip, wherever it takes you. In a similar dream, you may be trying to cross a river, via a boat or a bridge, to get to someone or something important on the other side.

Variations:

River dreams can introduce elements of danger as well—you might be navigating whitewater rapids, doing whatever it takes to avoid being cast into the rough waters. Rivers can also easily overflow during storms, and trying to cross a swollen, raging river can be deadly, if you are swept away by the currents.

The Spin:
???

A river's current flows in one direction, and as such, rivers have long been common means of transportation. According to dream analyst Gillian Holloway, in the same way that a highway can represent the road of life, a river represents the flow that our lives take. The water imagery introduces personal, unconscious qualities to the dream metaphor. In this way, it can signify a move toward greater emotional maturity. Depending on your life history and internal framework, this journey could be lazy and uneventful (an easy float down a babbling stream) or fraught with danger and psychic trauma (a wild whitewater ride that threatens drowning at every turn).

Dreams of crossing a river often symbolize the challenges one must face before achieving a goal. This could involve making peace with people or experiences from your past or persevering in the face of obstacles in your path (metaphorically speaking, a current that tries to divert you from your true course).

What Freud Would Say:

In *The Interpretation of Dreams*, Freud argued that water images evoked memories of the womb and birth and regressive thoughts of childhood. Dreams in which the water, in whatever form, turned sinister could indicate anxiety about sex and repression of forbidden thoughts of bed-wetting.

What Jung Would Say:

Water is often representative of feminine energy (the Anima), and symbolizes the mystery of the unconscious. Powerful bodies of water are archetypal symbols for the collective unconscious. In his work *Dreams*, Jung also hinted that dreams of traveling down a river reflected the process of individuation, of knowing the self.

Cultural Context:

Mark Twain's *The Adventures of Huckleberry Finn*, in addition to being one of the first great American novels, is also an excellent metaphoric example of a river journey as a path to enlightenment. The 1885 story begins as an innocuous adventure: Huck Finn runs away to escape his opportunistic, alcoholic father, who beats Huck and tries to steal his money.

He meets up with Jim, an escaped slave, and together they travel down the Mississippi River in a mutual quest for emancipation. Along the way they encounter various con men and criminals, as well as people with good hearts. The river in this story is both an avenue for escape and an introduction to society's moral as well as unsavory aspects. Huck's emotional journey ends with a bitter, resigned awareness of the hypocrisy and racism he encountered on the river trip, and he decides, at the end of the novel, to turn his back on civilization and head for the unexplored West.

Related Images: Beach/Ocean (p. 28); Desert Island (p. 81); Drowning/Breathing Underwater (p. 84)

71. 📷 **ROOMS, SECRET**

Common Manifestations: You are wandering through a building of some sort when you stumble upon a room, or group of rooms, that you did not expect to be there. Perhaps you tripped a mechanism that opened a secret panel in the wall; or you walked by the same door, day after day, and forgot the rooms were there; or the rooms might have just inexplicably appeared. Regardless, their presence is a delightful and curious surprise as you enter this new realm and begin to explore.

Variations:	The more ominous type of secret-room dream is that of a locked room that looms large in your consciousness. You know it's there, but its presence unnerves you. You might fight to get the door open or stay away in fear.
The Spin:	Rooms in a house usually represent individual aspects of the dreamer's personality. Rooms that mysteriously appear as a happy surprise evoke the great untapped potential that lies within. The unconscious mind is encouraging you to fulfill your potential, to rediscover your talents—get in there, clean out the junk, and showcase this new part of yourself with pride.
	And then there's the scary type of secret-room dream. This common dream visual represents something different for each individual. What's behind your locked door? Some people worry that this dream hints at repressed memories of abuse. Not necessarily. Often, your unconscious simply perceives danger in acknowledging certain feelings or realities, and it seeks to divert attention or scare you off from exploring issues that might cause short-term pain. According to dream analyst Gillian Holloway, the key to unlocking your scary secret-room dream is patience and self-compassion—in time, your anxiety may dwindle, and you'll catch a glimpse of what lies on the other side of the door.
What Freud Would Say:	In *The Interpretation of Dreams*, Freud stated, "Rooms in dreams are usually women; if the various ways in

and out of them are represented, this interpretation is scarcely open to doubt." He made some equally oblique comments about the symbolism behind keys and keyholes as they relate to unlocking a room and finding the way inside. Not one to leave any sexual stone unturned, he also argued that a "dream of going through a suite of rooms is a brothel or harem dream."

What Jung Would Say: According to the Jungian dream analysis Web site mythsdreamssymbols.com, a house represents the dreamer, and the state of the house represents one's relationship to the Self. So stumbling upon a room you didn't know was there could indicate that you have strengths and talents that have been heretofore unexpressed.

Cultural Context: For most people, secret rooms have a purely metaphoric resonance, but such hidden chambers had practical uses in days of old. Royal families and the societies surrounding palace courts were perpetual hotbeds of intrigue, betrayal, and assassination. Secret passages were hidden out of necessity: They were vital corridors for bearing assailants away, conducting assignations, and planning coups d'état. The Royal Pavilion in Brighton, England—one-time home to George IV, the Prince of Wales—is said to have secret tunnels that stretch to a mansion in nearby Old Steine, where George's mistress, Maria Fitzherbert, lived. The prince was forbidden to wed Fitzherbert, a Catholic, but they married in secret anyway and were reputed to have traveled back and forth through the tunnels until years later, when the prince's father, King George III, forced them to divorce so the prince could marry a Protestant (Catholics were barred from becoming queen).

Related Images: Basement (p. 26); Drowning/Breathing Underwater (p. 84); Rooms, Unused (p. 202); Treasure, Buried (p. 222)

72. 📷 **ROOMS, UNUSED**

Common Manifestations: In your dream, you are wandering through a house. The house may be familiar, or one you have never encountered. As you explore, you come upon one or several unused rooms in the house, forgotten and empty.

Variations: It could be that instead of finding an empty room, you've happened upon a room that you didn't even realize was there.

Occurrence: ♀ Dream dictionary author Sandra Thomson believes that dreams of empty or unused rooms may characterize the onset of menopause.

The Spin: 💚 ☠ The house is a very personal, immediate dream symbol, one which can evoke a specific time in someone's life, but which can also serve as a metaphor for the self. Particular rooms of a house, and the function of those rooms, often reflect a particular aspect of the dreamer's personality. Sandra Thomson argues that unused or empty rooms may symbolize feelings that have withered or died about a relationship in your life.

On the other hand, rooms that mysteriously appear as a happy surprise evoke the great untapped potential that lies within. Your unconscious mind is encouraging you to fulfill your potential, to rediscover your talents—get in there, clean out the junk, and showcase this new part of yourself with pride.

What Freud Would Say: In *The Interpretation of Dreams*, Freud stated, "Rooms in dreams are usually women; if the various ways in and out of them are represented, this interpretation is scarcely open to doubt." He made several equally oblique comments about the symbolism behind keys and keyholes as they relate to unlocking a room and finding the way inside. Not one to leave any sexual stone unturned, he also argued that a "dream of going through a suite of rooms is a brothel or harem dream."

What Jung Would Say: The house is a metaphor for the Self. Through dreaming, you will learn about aspects of the Self that you have previously repressed or obscured. So by discovering these "unused" parts of the house, you have achieved greater awareness of who you are and what you are capable of.

Related Images: Attic (p. 24); Basement (p. 26); Corridors/Hallways
                   (p. 64); Home, Childhood (p. 136); Kitchen (p. 151);
                   Rooms, Secret (p. 199)

---

73. 🔘   **SEX, GENDER REVERSAL**

Common   If you are a heterosexual, you dream of a passionate
Manifestations: same-sex encounter with someone you are not attracted
                to in waking life. This dream also applies to gay men
                or women who dream of a passionate heterosexual
                experience.

Variations: You dream that you are a member of the opposite sex,
                with the genitalia and secondary sex characteristics to
                prove it.

Occurrence: According to psychologist Alan Siegel, expectant
♂   fathers commonly dream of homosexual encounters.

The Spin: As with other sex dreams, imagining an encounter with
♡ ???   a member of the sex you are not normally attracted to
                doesn't necessarily mean that you harbor doubts about
                your own sexuality. Usually, sex is a dream metaphor
                that symbolizes other types of connections between
                people, or the yin/yang balance within your own psy-
                che. Try to zero in on the personality of your dream
                lover and the tenor of your dream experience. If it's
                a positive dream, perhaps you want to emulate the

qualities of your imagined lover. If the dream provokes anxiety, you might be ambivalent about exhibiting the dream lover's traits in your waking life. Similarly, dreaming you are a member of the opposite sex can indicate you are curious to explore other aspects of the self, or that you have recently undergone a significant change in your perspective on life.

What Freud Would Say:	Homosexual dream imagery is an expression of your guilt over latent sexual feelings.
What Jung Would Say:	Dreams of homosexuality represent a psychic imbalance of either masculine or feminine energy. The same-sex other in your dream could also symbolize your Shadow self—like a negative photographic image, the parts of your personality that have yet to arrive in the forefront of your consciousness.
Cultural Context:	Jung's notion of merging with your Shadow self, or confronting your dark side, has sparked some compelling storylines, from Oscar Wilde's *The Picture of Dorian Gray* to the Batman comic books to the *Star Wars* series. Perhaps the most overt artistic examination of this duality is Robert Louis Stevenson's *The Strange Case of Dr. Jekyll and Mr. Hyde*.
Related Images:	Sex with Someone You Know (Not Your Partner) (p. 211)

74. **SEX, INTERRUPTED/NOWHERE TO MAKE LOVE**

Common
Manifestations:

In the middle of a passionate sexual encounter with your partner, someone you know barges in with a pressing question or request. The intruder—perhaps your boss or a parent—seems unfazed at interrupting you during an intimate moment.

Variations:

In a similar dream, you and your partner are extremely amorous, but can't find a private place to consummate your passion. In every secret place you find, people suddenly appear; or perhaps a nagging responsibility distracts you from your tryst.

The Spin:

These kinds of dreams give voice to internal frustration. It's unlikely that the dream is literal or prophetic—your unconscious is not showing you how one single person or event is standing in the way of happiness for you and your partner. Instead, this story line usually hints at the kind of intangible obstacles that can lead to relationship roadblocks. What keeps you from making an emotional connection with your partner? Is it something within— a fear of intimacy? Or is another relationship in your life—with a friend, a family member—too intrusive or smothering, distracting you from your love match?

If Recurrent:

Your relationship frustration—or hesitation—is considerable. Deal with it!

What Freud Would Say:	The principle of wish fulfillment would imply that you have an unconscious desire to be observed having sex— or, to have sex with the person who interrupts you.
What Jung Would Say:	Sex, for Jung, symbolized a union of the masculine and feminine energies in each person's nature; it was this synthesis and balance of opposing forces that account for developmental progression. When dreams focus on the inability to connect with a partner, it's a sign that your energies are out of balance and that other, unconscious behaviors have gained prominence.
Cultural Context:	In Greek mythology, Zeus, randy ruler of Mount Olympus, regularly pursued and impregnated mortal women; his wife, Hera, employed endless, creative methods to interrupt or thwart these consummations. Zeus turned Io into a cow to escape detection, and Hera, hip to his ruse, took the beast as a gift, placing the bovine under the watchful one hundred eyes of Argus, so Zeus could not get near her. Callisto, another of Zeus's conquests, caused such jealousy that Hera turned the young maid into a bear. And when the lovely Leda caught Zeus's eye, he turned himself into a swan before seducing her to escape Hera's scrutiny. Surprisingly, Zeus's nonhuman state didn't stop Leda from taking him as a lover. Talk about a couple in desperate need of counseling.
Related Images:	Animals (p. 21); Sex in Public (p. 208)

75. 📷   **SEX IN PUBLIC**

Common
Manifestations: You and your partner are overcome by passion. Only
after you are deeply involved in an erotic encounter
do you discover that you are both in full view in an
excessively public place. Though you are embarrassed
by the spectacle, no one else seems to notice.

Variations: As you and your partner have sex, you notice that
your parents, or some other authority figure (your boss,
a teacher, a police officer), are watching everything
you do.

Occurrence: This dream could occur if you have recently started a
relationship with someone your friends or family might
view with disapproval—for example, someone of
another race, religion, or culture (if your family and
friends might find that shocking), or if you have
recently "come out" about a same-sex relationship.

The Spin: In this case, "sex in public" can be taken almost liter-
♡ ???   ally. You feel exposed and anxious about conducting a
relationship under what you perceive to be intense
scrutiny, and you are uncomfortable with the idea that
others might be talking about you and your "business."
However, if in the dream, no one notices you having
sex, that's a good sign your self-consciousness is
unwarranted, and that friends and family are simply
watching your life unfold, not sitting in judgment of

your lifestyle choice. If in your dream your parents are watching you copulate, then in waking life perhaps acting in opposition to your parents' values has unconsciously inhibited your ability to connect with a partner.

What Freud Would Say:

Two words: wish fulfillment (p. 255).

What Jung Would Say:

Sex often represents a merging of opposing energies or qualities within yourself, as a way to achieve greater inner balance. And sometimes, dreaming of sex is simply a straight-up expression of your desire.

Cultural Context:

Pagan fertility cults and ritual sex worship were common among the ancient Mesopotamian civilizations of Sumeria, Babylonia, Phoenicia, and Canaan. In Babylonia, temples to Ishtar—goddess of sexual power, fertility, birth, and all things female—were staffed with "sacred" prostitutes who had sex with worshippers that came to celebrate the fertility of nature and ensure the abundance of their crops. This practice persisted, in various forms, all the way through the cultures of ancient Egypt and Greece.

In modern-day Western society, public displays of sexual activity are not generally considered acceptable adult behavior. For some quarters of the gay male community, impersonal sex in restrooms and bathhouses is common practice—what sociologist Laud Humphreys called, in a 1970 book, the "tearoom trade." Adventurous paramours might have many motivations for having sex in public—thrilled at the risk of getting caught, carried away in the heat of the moment, or perhaps a desire to celebrate the scenery. Reuters recently reported that the mayor of small-town Spaarnwoude, Netherlands, has imported herds of cows to graze in the local nature preserve as a way to deter (and hopefully dampen the ardor) of the reportedly large number of couples who visit the preserve and have open-air sex.

Hollywood has long tested the boundaries of social outrage with its depiction of on-screen sex—in fact, films released in the early days of moving pictures were surprisingly risqué. Before the adoption of the Hays Code (stringent guidelines that until 1968 censored the depiction of sex, drugs, nudity, and other taboos), filmmakers tackled controversial subjects and erotic material without apology. Marlene Dietrich was notorious for such early roles as a sadomasochistic Catherine the Great in 1934's *The Scarlet Empress*. Although first drafted in 1927, the Hays Code was not enforced with vigor until 1934, which many believe was in direct response to the first mainstream movie to show intercourse: *Ecstasy*, a 1933 Czecho-slovakian drama starring the then-unknown actress Hedy Lamarr.

Related Images: Nudity, Public (p. 175)

76. **SEX WITH SOMEONE YOU KNOW (NOT YOUR PARTNER)**

Common Manifestations:
You are having sex with someone in your life who is not your partner—a good friend, a coworker, an ex, a passing acquaintance, even a friend's spouse. You might not be attracted to this person at all in waking life, but that doesn't stop you from pursuing your passion in the dream.

Variations:
This notion can also encompass disturbing incest dreams, in which you are having sex with a member of your family.

Occurrence:
In early adulthood, dreams are often role-playing scenarios during which you try different behaviors, partners, and characteristics on for size. You're learning what works for you, what will make you happy. After middle age, your dreams more likely take the form of memories, as you reflect on missed chances, great successes, and the things you cherish most—and so you might find yourself dreaming of your first love, or your "favorite mistake," or the one who got away.

The Spin:
It's possible to take the dream of sex with someone you know at face value, as either an expression of your own secret passions or your unconscious homing in on a latent attraction harbored by the other person. Try the gut-check test: Do you really think the person

you're dreaming about has a secret crush on you? Or that you have unacknowledged feelings in return? If so, and if your life circumstances prevent you from acting on those urges, then the dream sex is your unconscious pursuing an acceptable outlet for those feelings.

More often than not, it's a mistake to interpret such dreams literally. In the dream world, sexual imagery often stands in for the many types of connections that two people might share. Think of what the person in your dreams represents to you—a quality, a goal, an accomplishment, a problem—and whether that quality or issue preoccupies your thoughts in the here and now. If you find your dream partner distasteful, think about what it is that turns you off—and whether that nugget of unpleasantness is something you're experiencing in another area of your life.

Dreams of incest are unlikely to be a symptom of repressed childhood abuse. Instead, the connection your unconscious is making may be more complex and metaphorical. Your current partner might simply share a significant personality trait with a family member, and in real life you find yourself responding to him or her with the same old behavior patterns. Or perhaps the dream indicates that your relationship with your family is too "close"—not in a sexual way, but in a gossipy, in-each-other's-business, disrespectful-of-boundaries way.

What Freud Would Say:	One could argue that the Oedipus complex—that men unconsciously want to have sex with their mothers and spend a great deal of psychic energy repressing that realization—was Freud's bread and butter, the central hypothesis of his psychoanalytic theory. The same urge in women—the unconscious wish to have sex with their fathers—was called the Electra complex. Freud himself would probably say that your waking-life dream censors may prevent you from remembering any dreams of having sex with a parent, but that many other remembered dreams are really disguised wishes to have sex with a parent.
What Jung Would Say:	Having sex with someone other than your partner could indicate a secret desire or unhappiness in a current relationship. Or the dream partner could represent a part of your psyche you're having trouble assimilating. In the ideal Jungian world, sex symbolizes the union of male energy (the Animus) with female energy (the Anima); through this union the dreamer achieves inner balance. So the dream of having sex with another person could properly be understood as an invitation to increase your self-knowledge.
Cultural Context:	The Oedipus myth is one of the oldest morality tales in the world, popularized by Sophocles in the tragedy *Oedipus Rex*. Laius, king of Thebes, arranges for a shepherd to kill his newborn son to circumvent a prophecy

that the son would put his life and his throne in danger. But a peasant rescues and raises the boy, known as Oedipus. As an adult, Oedipus, during a roadside altercation, slays two strangers, one of them the king, his biological father. Shortly thereafter, the citizens of Thebes make Oedipus their king when he saves them from the Sphinx. He marries Jocasta, the queen, unaware that she is his biological mother. When pestilence strikes the city, the oracle at Delphi proclaims that Thebes will not recover until Laius's murderer is expelled from town. Upon investigating, Oedipus discovers the truth about his parentage and the prophecies surrounding him. Jocasta hangs herself in shame, and Oedipus, horrified, stabs out his eyes and wanders in exile for the rest of his days.

The story of Electra appears in the work of Sophocles (*Electra*) and Aeschylus (*The Libation Bearers*), among others. Electra was the daughter of Clytemnestra and Agamemnon. After Agamemnon returned from fighting the Trojan War, Clytemnestra conspired with her lover, Aegisthus, to murder her husband. Electra was so outraged and grief-stricken that she helped her brother, Orestes, avenge their father's murder by killing both their mother and her murderous lover.

Related Images: Father (p. 109); Infidelity (p. 142); Mother (p. 163)

77.   SEX WITH STRANGER

Common
Manifestations:
You are having satisfying and uninhibited sex; the sensations are intensely erotic and feel very real. But your partner is someone unfamiliar, someone you don't recognize.

Variations:
In the middle of your erotic encounter, you notice that your partner has no face. Or, as the encounter progresses, you find your partner dissolving or vanishing into the air, like a ghost.

Occurrence:
This type of dream is common during early adulthood, at a time when you might be preoccupied with finding the right partner. This dream could also arise when you are single and unattached.

The Spin:
This is a great dream to have. Your lover's lack of identity removes interpersonal tension from the dream equation and frees you to focus wholly on the sexual experience. In this way, you're learning what stimulates you and what type of partner suits you best. The guest star in your dream might not even be a person at all but may simply represent a specific character trait or quality that you are looking for in a mate. If you are romantically unattached at the time you have this dream, it may also indicate a willingness to jump back into the relationship waters.

♡???   However, if your dream lover is of the ghostlike, vanishing variety, this may be a signal that you're not getting what you need from your present partner. It might indicate frustrations in a current relationship. In this case, it's important to pinpoint what the dream lover delivers that you're not getting in waking life.

If Recurrent: Your unconscious is giving you a road map to your sexual preferences or encouraging you to be receptive to a new relationship.

What Freud Would Say: Freud argued that dreams with overtly sexual content are unconsciously traumatizing to the conscious mind, and as a result the mind represses the true "meaning" of the dream by employing seemingly innocuous or irrelevant dream imagery. In that sense, all dreams are representational, their meanings disguised by an internal censoring he called the dream work. In fact, in *The Interpretation of Dreams*, he went so far as to assert, "It is fair to say that there is no group of ideas that is incapable of representing sexual facts and wishes." (Translation: Sometimes a cigar is not just a cigar.)

What Jung Would Say: This type of dream might symbolically represent the union of the halves of the Self—the Anima (feminine side) with the Animus (masculine side). And the stranger in the dream may well represent aspects of your psyche you have yet to explore or understand.

| Cultural Context: | Sex with strangers can happen even within the confines of traditional monogamy. In cultures where marriages are arranged, the couple might only meet for the first time on their wedding day. And in certain over-whelmingly male-populated regions of the American West and Northwest, mail-order brides were once a common phenomenon. |

Many a song has been fashioned around the imaginary or unknown lover; the dream lover who never disappoints has been a fixture in such movies as 1987's *Making Mr. Right*, with Ann Magnuson and John Malkovich.

Greek mythology gives us the cautionary tale of Cupid and Psyche. Cupid took Psyche as his wife, set her up in a posh palace with servants and riches galore, but came to her only at night, not allowing her to see him or to know his identity. Curiosity eventually got the better of her, and one night while Cupid slept she lit a candle to gaze upon his face, finding not the monster she feared but a beautiful god. Cupid flew away, upset at Psyche's betrayal, saying, "Love cannot dwell with suspicion." They reunited eventually, after Psyche endured several trials at the hands of her vengeful mother-in-law, Venus.

| Related Images: | Communication Breakdown (p. 55); Infidelity (p. 142); Sex in Public (p. 208) |

78.   **SWAMP**

Common
Manifestations:

You find yourself in a swamp, either tromping in the muck or floating among the reeds and mangroves. It's hard to breathe through the humidity, and even harder to find your way through the many twists and turns the swamp takes. Getting lost isn't your only problem. You're surrounded by wildlife, and not the sweet, fluffy kind, either. Is that a water moccasin over there? Or, god forbid, an alligator?

Variations:

You might not be lost, but you may well be stuck—tangled in a web of vines or sinking slowly into quicksand.

The Spin:
???

Although a thriving ecosystem in its own right, a swamp is a place characterized by stale, stagnant water—an apt dream metaphor when you're feeling stuck in a rut or without motivation to effect change in your waking life. You could be uncertain over the next step to take (hence the tangled vines holding you in place) or you might simply be "stuck" in an old way of thinking that doesn't do justice to your wants and needs. Perhaps a love or family relationship is dragging you down, keeping you from making progress? Quicksand (p. 169) has similar swampy qualities with an added twist of surprise: Those quicksand pits appear out of nowhere, when you least expect them.

If Recurrent:	Purchase a good mosquito repellent, and if you see an alligator, keep your arms and legs inside the boat.
What Freud Would Say:	For Freud, the murky, impenetrable swamp was a fitting metaphor for the mysteries of the unconscious mind. In *The Interpretation of Dreams*, he argued that water images evoked memories of the womb and birth and regressive thoughts of childhood. Dreams in which the water has sinister qualities could indicate anxiety about sex and repression of forbidden thoughts of bed-wetting.
What Jung Would Say:	Water is often representative of feminine energy (the Anima) and symbolizes the mystery of the unconscious. Deep, murky bodies of water were archetypal symbols for the collective unconscious. In his work *Dreams*, Jung hinted that the more primitive and "natural" a dream environment, the more likely that environment reflects the mother archetype.
Related Images:	Drowning/Breathing Underwater (p. 84); Jungle (p. 148); Lost, Being (p. 155); Mud (p. 169); Paralysis/Running in Slow Motion (p. 178)

79.   **TEETH FALLING OUT**

Common Manifestations:	You are going about your everyday business when you suddenly taste blood in your mouth. A tooth has come

loose, and as you reach up to your lips, it falls out and you spit it into your hand. Alarmed, you soon feel one tooth after the other separating from your gums, as you struggle to staunch the blood and save the teeth.

Variations: Your teeth crumble out of your open mouth like broken cookies.

Occurrence: This dream is likely to occur during middle age, at times of great responsibility, and perhaps as you enter senior citizenship.

The Spin: This surprisingly common dream has little to do with dental phobia. In this case, your teeth are a metaphoric signpost for times of great life change. Baby teeth fall out as you enter adolescence, and wisdom teeth come in as you become an adult. The onset of old age goes hand in hand with the deterioration of your teeth. So losing your teeth can be understood as an expression of insecurity at the prospect of upcoming change. The shame and embarrassment associated with the loss of your teeth can also parallel feelings of inadequacy or lack of confidence during times of stress.

If Recurrent: Maybe it's time for a cleaning and checkup. And make sure to floss regularly.

What Freud Would Say: Dreams "with a dental stimulus" reflect a desire for masturbation in both men and women. Additionally, for men, the missing-teeth dream expresses a fear of castration. Although the connection between penis and teeth may seem entirely arbitrary, Freud believed that sexual repression in the dreamer caused a "transposition" of the penis anxiety (in the lower part of the body) into dental anxiety (in the upper part of the body). Freud also believed that, for women, the dream of losing teeth symbolized a desire to have children.

What Jung Would Say:

A dream of losing your teeth indicates that you are anxious about losing power and vitality as you age.

Cultural Context:

According to Gayle Delaney, author of *In Your Dreams*, the losing-your-teeth dream casts a long shadow throughout history. First mention can be traced all the way back to the Chester Beatty papyrus, an ancient Egyptian dream manual dating from 2000 BCE. Here, the loss of one's teeth augurs the dreamer's murder by his family. The Talmud records a similar prophecy: Dream of losing your teeth, and expect a death in the family. The Greek scholar Artemidorus—perhaps the world's first dream expert—wrote a book in 200 CE that examined the dream interpretation traditions of ancient Greece and Rome. In it, he presents teeth as a metaphor for social standing. If you dream of losing your teeth, he claims, you will lose power and possessions. But conversely, if a slave dreams of losing his teeth, he will soon win his freedom.

Related Images: Exam/Public Performance (p. 101); Lost, Being
(p. 155); Mouth and Teeth (p. 166); Nudity, Public
(p. 175); Purse or Wallet, Lost (p. 193)

---

80. **TREASURE, BURIED**

Common
Manifestations:

As happy dreams go, it's hard to beat one in which you
discover buried treasure. You might literally stumble
upon money, jewels, coins, or other riches while walking
along the street, on the beach, or in the wilderness.
Or perhaps you discover a windfall that has been
tucked away in your house all along. Most people
report that, in the dream, they know intuitively the
treasure is meant for them to keep—although occasionally such a dream inspires anxiety that the discovery
implies "stealing" from the rightful owner.

Variations: In a similar dream, some ordinary object in your day-
to-day life becomes a talisman imbued with magical
properties.

Occurrence: This is a common dream among highly creative and
artistic people.

The Spin: Although it's irresistible to think this dream might
foretell the future, the dream meaning probably points
to assets that are more psychological than material.
The treasure is a metaphor for unacknowledged or

latent talents you might harbor. (Jewels in particular often symbolize a special or higher knowledge.) If the dream treasure is "buried," these talents may be hidden or suppressed in your day-to-day life. Similarly, if an ordinary object suddenly exhibits magic properties, then perhaps your real-life "treasure" is hiding in plain sight, waiting to be identified.

If Recurrent: Having this dream on a regular basis indicates that you may be struggling with questions about the direction your life will take. Are you stuck in an old way of looking at things? This dream is asking you to take a step back and reassess where you are and what you want to do. In doing so, you might better understand what you're searching for and how best to capitalize on your as-yet unrealized talents. The answer—and the treasure—lies within.

What Freud Would Say: Freud felt that excrement and defecation (in short, anal imagery) symbolized money; they represented humanity's first attempt to expend effort in order to produce something tangible, and they triggered feelings of pride, aggression, and shame. In *The Interpretation of Dreams*, he stated, "Dreams with an intestinal stimulus throw light in an analogous fashion on the symbolism involved in them and at the same time confirm the connection between gold and feces, which is also supported by copious evidence from social anthropology."

What Jung
Would Say:

Jung believed that buried treasure was a frequent metaphor for the Self, and in particular that part of the Self that stays hidden, that we struggle to know and understand. He also believed that such archetypal mythological imagery—the hero, the quest, the treasure—were so far removed from the "banalities of everyday" because they speak to "a part of the personality which has not yet come into existence but is still in the process of becoming."

Cultural
Context:

Dreams of finding money or treasure weren't always considered harbingers of positive self-discovery. The ancient Greek dream interpreter Artemidorus, in his seminal work *Oneirocritica*, stated, "Some men maintain that money and all kinds of coins indicate bad luck, but I have observed that small coins and copper coins mean discontent and painful exchanges of words." And according to Gustavus Hindman Miller, author of a popular dream dictionary published in the early twentieth century, "To dream you find a roll of currency, and a young woman claims it, foretells that you will lose in some enterprises by the interference of some female friend. The dreamer will find that he is spending his money unwisely and is living beyond his means. It is a dream of caution. Beware, lest the innocent fancies of your brain make a place for your money before payday."

Related Images: Drowning/Breathing Underwater (p. 84); Purse or Wallet, Lost (p. 193)

81. **TUNNEL**

Common
Manifestations:

You are traveling through a tunnel, either on foot or in a vehicle. The walls and ceiling hug you close; there's not a lot of room to move. You might be running away from something (escaping a dangerous situation) or moving toward something you can't quite see. No matter how dark the tunnel is, a light beckons you from the end.

Occurrence:

Dreams of tunnel travel often arise during times of great life change—birth, death, retirement, and so on.

The Spin:

Tunnels are methods of transport that carry you from one place to another, allowing you to pass through immovable objects (mountains) or dangerous environments (rivers or other large bodies of water). As such, they can symbolize a life in transition; you're on the move. That journey could be external (changing careers, starting a family, ending a marriage) or internal (healing old emotional wounds, exploring psychic obstacles to your success). At the moment, you can't see your destination, but you know your life will be very different once you arrive.

??? The character of a tunnel is closed in, with limited space to navigate; this can represent a kind of single-minded perspective (or tunnel vision). You can only see where you're going or where you've been—there's no room for nuance in your life. But such limitation can also be comforting. A small, enclosed tunnel is a great place to hide from the demands of everyday life, and as such, it often symbolizes a desire to return to the safety and protection of the womb, if only for a brief time.

What Freud Would Say: As dark places that transport you to the light, tunnels are, along with caves, classic Freudian symbols of the vagina. In one of Freud's more single-entendre moments, he stated that the image of a train hurtling through a tunnel is a common dream depiction of intercourse.

What Jung Would Say: Tunnels, similar to caves, are dark places that harbor the secrets of the unconscious. Jung was mindful of the hopeful character of the tunnel, which by its very nature transports one closer to the "light," that is, greater self-knowledge.

Related Images: Cave (p. 43); Lost, Being (p. 155); Mud (p. 169)

82. **VEHICLE THAT ISN'T A VEHICLE**

Common Manifestations: In this offbeat dream, you find yourself traveling from one place to another in something that wasn't meant for conveyance. You could be piloting a bathtub, a giant soup pot, an office desk, or even a washing machine as you zoom down the road. You may be stumped about how to navigate, but your ersatz vehicle is nevertheless taking you where you intend to go.

Variations: Maybe your means of dream transport isn't logical, but the way you are utilizing the transport is: You're sailing a submarine down the highway or driving a car across the ocean.

The Spin: According to dream analyst Gillian Holloway, the key
🎗 ??? to understanding this dream is to discover any waking-life associations you have for these makeshift vehicles. Do you dream of traveling via stockpot because you're starting up a catering business? Is your washing-machine car a sign that you want to flee the perpetual demands of housework? Do you bring your work home with you, literally, by parking your desk in the garage? How well you commandeer the unusual vehicle is also significant. If you glide along with ease, maybe in real life you're on the right track, so to speak. But if the makeshift conveyance feels unsafe or in need of repair, it could be a sign that a waking-life coping mechanism isn't working for you.

What Freud Freud found most forms of transportation—whether
Would Say: automobiles, trains, or planes—not so subtly phallic in their symbolism. And he believed that perilous

dreams of crashing a strange vehicle could easily be interpreted as an expression of Thanatos, or the death wish, much as he believed dreams of missing a train (p. 61) were anxiety dreams about the fear of death.

What Jung Would Say:

In his book *Dreams*, Jung argued that the type of vehicle that appears in a transportation-related dream "illustrates the . . . manner in which the dreamer . . . lives his psychic life." Jung found significance in whether the method of transportation was individual or collective, self-propelled or mechanical. People traveling in airplanes, for example, are "flown by an unknown pilot" and "borne along on intuitions emanating from the unconscious." But a person who takes a dream ride on a tram or other public transportation "moves or behaves just like everybody else."

Related Images:

Accident with Airplane, Train, Car, or Boat (p. 8); Airplane (p. 11); Boat (p. 36); Car Trouble/Driving Problems (p. 41); Connections, Missed (p. 61); Mechanical Malfunction (p. 158)

---

83.   **WAR ZONE**

Common Manifestations:

You find yourself on a battleground, war in every direction. The noise of bombs detonating and weapons firing fills your ears. People all around you are wounded or dead. Perhaps you merely observe the scene in horror, or you might be in the thick of it, engaged in hand-to-hand combat. Waking from the dream, you are at once frightened and relieved.

Variations: You could also be dreaming of an apocalyptic battle, one that presages the end of the world (p. 98).

The Spin: Dreaming of war is a fairly straightforward expression of conflict in your waking life. Perhaps you're staving off a hostile takeover at work, or you're at odds with a family member or spouse (remember what the great philosopher Pat Benatar once said: Love is a battle-field). Often, the battle you wage is internal, between opposing urges in your psyche. The key to defusing the hostility, no matter who or what is in conflict, is to recognize that it's not about one side winning or losing, but about both sides knowing that the most prudent course of action is to simply stop fighting and to make peace with the other.

If Recurrent: This could also be a posttraumatic dream, or reflect fear for a loved one who is currently serving in the military. If so, and if the dreams return with regularity, it's best to seek professional counseling.

What Freud Would Say: Freud believed that war was a fundamental expression of man's innate instinct toward hatred and aggression. In *The Interpretation of Dreams*, Freud described a dream reported by Napoleon I, who had fallen asleep in his carriage during the heat of battle. He woke up after a bomb exploded nearby, and reported dreaming of an entirely different battle. It was clear to Freud that Napoleon "wove the noise of an exploding bomb into the battle dream before he woke up from it." Freud used this anecdote to illustrate his theory that dreams help to prolong sleep, hence his famous quote: "Dreams are the guardians of sleep and not its disturbers."

What Jung
Would Say:

In his book *Dreams*, Jung described a straightforward war dream in terms of inner conflict, saying, "The conscious mind is trying to defend its position and suppress the unconscious."

Related Images:

Death of Loved One (Unrelated to Actual Death) (p. 73); Death, Your Own (p. 76); End of the World (p. 98); Weapons: Bombs, Clubs, Guns, and Knives (p. 233); Wounds (p. 236)

---

84. **WATER**

Common
Manifestations:

You are surrounded by water, in the ocean or in a deep lake. Perhaps you are sailing along on a boat or are floating through the water of your own volition. Despite your awareness of the depth and power of the water surrounding you, the feeling of drifting through the waves is soothing and peaceful.

Variations: This type of dream can have an ominous side as well. The water overwhelms you; you may be sucked underwater, in danger of drowning (p. 84), or the water inexorably pursues you, flooding your home, car, or neighborhood.

Occurrence: This dream might have a very straightforward physiological prompt: You could be thirsty, or a full bladder could be sending a not-so-subliminal message that you need to use the facilities. A flood dream might be a posttraumatic reenactment, or it could symbolize hydrophobia, a fear of swimming or deep water.

The Spin: Water is a powerful dream symbol, one that evokes
??? deep, often obscured emotions and can recall the amniotic fluid of a mother's womb. Deep bodies of water symbolize the unconscious: powerful, diverse, and largely hidden from view. Pay attention to the condition of the water in your dream. Is it clear or murky? Still or tempestuous? Vast or circumscribed? The state of the dream water could help you identify the nature of underlying emotions. Do you know yourself with clarity, or find yourself lost in a "sea of confusion"? Are you at peace with your thoughts, or are you buffeted by stormy thoughts? If you are plunging into a pool or find the dream water cleansing, you could be yearning for a spiritual healing—a baptism. Having grandiose water dreams also could suggest that your emotions,

intuition, and creativity are taking new precedence in your life.

If, however, the water in your dream turns ominous or life-threatening (and if you are not having a posttraumatic reaction to a real-life disaster), your waking-life emotions are likely highly volatile and potentially overwhelming. The sensation of struggling against—and being defeated by—a powerful force of nature is an apt metaphor for how overwhelmed you can feel by your emotions, or by a seemingly intractable situation. Think about how a tsunami, associated with the unforgiving ocean and underwater earthquakes, could sweep you away suddenly, without warning. Or how rising flood waters could inexorably swallow you, despite your attempts to control the overflow.

What Freud Would Say: Freud argued that water images evoked memories of the womb and birth and regressive thoughts of childhood. Dreams in which the water, in whatever form, turned sinister could indicate anxiety about sex and repression of forbidden thoughts of bed-wetting.

What Jung Would Say: Water is often representative of feminine energy (the Anima), and symbolizes the mystery of the unconscious. Large bodies of water, such as the oceans and seas, are archetypal symbols for the collective unconscious. Men who fear water in real life may harbor fears of women or of their emotional/feminine side.

Cultural Context: As essential as emotions are to our inner lives, so is water essential to life on Earth. More than seventy percent of Earth is covered by water (either fresh- or saltwater); the human body is approximately sixty percent water as well. Humans can go without food for three weeks or more but can only live without water for less than one week before perishing.

Related Images: Drowning/Breathing Underwater (p. 84); Mud (p. 169); Natural Disasters: Earthquakes, Hurricanes, Tornadoes, and Volcanoes (p. 172); Rain (p. 194)

85. ## WEAPONS: BOMBS, CLUBS, GUNS, AND KNIVES

Common Manifestations: Someone is brandishing a weapon at you, whether it be a gun, knife, staff, or explosive. The threat you feel is immediate and powerful, and anxiety makes your pulse race.

Variations: You could be the person wielding the weapon, or you could be engaged in some kind of hand-to-hand combat with a similarly armed assailant.

The Spin: Dreams that feature weapons—guns, knives, even military artillery—are expressions of aggression: your own toward someone else, someone else's toward you, or even your aggression toward a particular aspect of your own personality. As a sign of someone else's aggression toward you, this dream could be intended as a warning that you need to watch your back for possible betrayals or attacks. If you are wielding the weapon in the dream, who or what are you threatening? Identifying your intended victim could help you understand where your feelings of aggression are coming from.

Certain types of weapons have metaphoric meanings. Long, hard, sharp objects (swords, knives, bayonets, clubs) carry obvious phallic symbolism (see "What Freud Would Say," opposite), hinting at sexual issues—either aggression or fear of domination—that need addressing. According to dream analyst Gillian Holloway, guns represent a very masculine type of bullying force. If you have trouble finding or using a gun in your dream, you may be unsure about wielding power in a real-life situation. Knives symbolize an emotional hurt, and these wounds can cut you to the quick. A woman being chased by a knife-wielding man is a dream of sexual fear. Bullets, bombs, and grenades imply sudden, destructive explosions, emanating from a tension that escalated to dangerous levels. Does this parallel your waking life, in which you need to disarm a potentially explosive situation at work or in a relationship?

If Recurrent: Cancel your subscription to *Guns & Ammo*.

What Freud Would Say:	For Freud, dreams of weapons expressed sexual aggression (in males) or sexual insecurity (in females). Freud famously related the case history of a twenty-seven-year-old patient who dreamt that a man was chasing him with a hatchet. Through free association, the man remembered when he was nine years old and heard his parents having intercourse. The noises sounded violent and painful to him, a fact reinforced by blood he saw on their sheets the next day. In this case, Freud was able to draw a direct connection between sex and violence.
What Jung Would Say:	Dream dictionary author Sandra Thomson observes that for Jungian analysts, knives represent psychological insight—a peeling away of the superficial and a cutting to the heart of the matter. Any type of explosion could indicate that there is something in your unconscious that is screaming for release.
Cultural Context:	It has become a virtual cliché that men with big guns wield them as proof of their masculinity or in order to mask certain physical shortcomings. Certainly Hollywood reinforces that impression, from Clint Eastwood and Charles Bronson caressing their .45 Magnums in the *Dirty Harry* and *Death Wish* movies (interesting that Bronson's character sought to avenge the murder of his wife), to Joe Don Baker as ass-whuppin' Sheriff Buford Pusser in *Walking Tall*—with his big, smooth, destructive billy club. But perhaps

the most brutally obvious cinematic illustration of weapon as phallic stand-in has to be the giant pneumatic drill used to eviscerate a buxom woman in Brian De Palma's 1984 thriller *Body Double*.

Related Images: Crime, Committing (p. 66); Crime, Victim of (p. 70); End of the World (p. 98)

86. **WOUNDS**

Common Manifestations: You dream that you are wounded. The wound can be minor or catastrophic—maybe you nicked your finger on a carving knife, or you had a limb severed. The blood is noticeable, and the pain is persistent. Seeing that much blood makes your heart beat harder, and you may wake up feeling disoriented or panicked. Sometimes, in a loss-of-blood dream, a savior appears to offer a badly needed transfusion.

Variations: In a related dream, you may be traveling in a war zone (p. 228) when you happen upon a group of gravely wounded soldiers. Or you may dream of being covered in disfiguring, badly healed scars.

The Spin: Dream images that relate to your body are often
??? metaphoric substitutes for deep-seated emotions. So picturing yourself covered in scars—a wound that didn't heal properly or was grave enough to leave a

permanent mark—could shed light on some psychological pain that you're harboring. Expressions such as "I haven't got a leg to stand on," "I lost my head," and "I can't stomach his presence," are not intended literally but serve to drive an emotional point home. Severe wounds—losing a limb, internal bleeding—give voice to parts of the psyche that have been neglected or mistreated. A wound that has reopened after closing up is often a metaphor for the remembrance of an old hurt. A wound that involves a loss of blood could be interpreted as a lack of energy or gumption in your waking life. Is your job bleeding you dry? Has an unhealthy relationship or conflict sapped your strength? If you required a blood transfusion, who gave it? Maybe that person (or institution) is what will revitalize you.

If Recurrent: It's possible, though admittedly not likely, that multiple or repeated dreams of being wounded could be your unconscious hinting at the onset of an illness.

What Freud Would Say: Freud and several of his followers posited something called the birth trauma, or the devastating effect of being born on every human being—of being pushed through the narrow, dark, suffocating birth canal in order to arrive in the world. Freud believed that the birth trauma could not be understood or accepted but must be repressed. Interesting, then, to note that *trauma* is the Greek word for "wound"—something that is so difficult for the body to assimilate that it leaves a mark, a scar.

What Jung Would Say: According to the Jungian dream interpretation Web site mythsdreamssymbols.com, blood is the source of life, love, and spirituality. Dreaming of a wound, of losing your blood, could symbolize a drain on your emotions or on any psychological weakness that needs addressing. Dreaming of drinking someone else's blood is an overt metaphor for drawing upon another's strength. Dreaming of menstrual blood could symbolize sexual anxiety for both men and women.

Cultural Context: Dreaming of wounds in a purely metaphoric fashion speaks, in an oblique way, to the luxury of medical developments in modern society. In a world of first-aid creams, hydrogen peroxide, and antibiotics, it's easy to forget that infections from the smallest cuts were often fatal to even the hardiest of humans. Until the invention of penicillin and other antibiotics in the early part of the twentieth century, wounds—especially war wounds—were almost always fatal because of the rapid onset of staph and other bacterial infections.

Related Images: Crime, Victim of (p. 70); War Zone (p. 228); Weapons: Bombs, Clubs, Guns, and Knives (p. 233)

Glossary

Adler, Alfred (1870–1937): Psychiatrist, one-time disciple of Freud, and founder of what has come to be known as individual psychology, or cognitive therapy. Adler took a rational approach to the personality, believing that people yearned for community and that the greatest challenge faced by the human psyche was to grapple with feelings of inferiority (Adler was the first to use the term *inferiority complex*). He argued for a holistic theory of dreams, believing that a dream's meaning was entirely personal, dependent on the particular circumstances and the value of particular symbols in a dreamer's life. For him, psychotherapy was a "reeducation" process, in which a patient examined, and attempted to overcome, any internal feelings of inferiority. *See also* **Freud, Sigmund**.

Aesculapius: The Greek god of healing, said to be responsible for the content and quality of dreams. Temples throughout the ancient Greek world honored Aesculapius; people seeking advice or medical help would wait for a "dream invitation" from the gods to visit the temple. Once there, they presented offerings and slept in the temple until Aesculapius (or one of his attendants) appeared in a dream with the necessary guidance. *See also* **Imhotep; Incubation**.

Amplification: For Jung, the process by which an individual arrived at the personal meaning of a dream. In his analyses, Jung asked patients to begin with the simple statement of a dream ("I dreamed of a red and white tablecloth"), and to "amplify" that statement by investigating the personal meaning of that symbol, and how it links to the dreamer's waking life ("My grandmother had a red and white tablecloth, and it reminds me of the happy times I spent with her during childhood summers").

Through amplification, Jung hoped to arrive at collective or archetypal dream meanings as well. *See also **Archetypes; Collective Unconscious; Jung, Carl Gustav**.*

Anima: For Jung, the archetypal feminine life force within the soul, representative of the "feminine" aspects of the male personality (intuition, introspection, emotion). The Anima might be represented in dreams as an earth mother, the Virgin Mary, or a Wise Old Woman. Some contemporary Jungian analysts have shied away from the Anima/Animus concept, given that it relies on culturally traditional (some might say sexist) definitions of male and female behavior. *See also **Animus; Archetypes; Individuation; Jung, Carl Gustav**.*

Animus: For Jung, the archetypal masculine life force within the soul, representative of the "masculine" aspects of the female personality (action, analytic ability, conviction). The Animus might be represented in dreams as a father figure or a Wise Old Man. Some contemporary Jungian analysts have shied away from the Anima/Animus concept, given that it relies on culturally traditional (some might say sexist) definitions of male and female behavior. *See also **Anima; Archetypes; Individuation; Jung, Carl Gustav**.*

Archetypes: The language or template employed by the unconscious mind to express personal as well as universal wisdom. Jung identified four primary archetypes: the **Anima/Animus**, the **Persona**, the **Self**, and the **Shadow**. *See also **Jung, Carl Gustav**.*

Artemidorus (c. second century CE): Ancient Greek author of *Oneirocritica*, one of the earliest recorded works of dream interpretation. Artemidorus believed that all dreams fell into two categories: those that were entirely frivolous and without significance and those that predicted the future. Unlike his contemporaries, who believed that dreams were straightforward messages from the gods regarding health and well-being, Artemidorus developed a great appreciation for how dreams communicated via metaphors that were highly personal to the dreamer—an insight that predates similar groundbreaking work by Sigmund Freud almost 1,800 years later. *See also* **Freud, Sigmund**.

Astral Projection: The belief that the soul can separate from the body and travel independently through this and other worlds. In many Native American, African, East Asian, and indigenous Australian cultures, the soul is thought to take long journeys while the body is asleep, and dreams are the slide shows from those travels.

Bes: In ancient Egypt, the god believed to protect people, both alive and dead, from danger. Because Egyptians believed that evil spirits were wont to visit them at night, especially while they were asleep, Bes was also thought to keep bad dreams at bay. *See also* **Imhotep**; **Incubation**.

Big Dream: For Jung, a dream that transcended the personal to incorporate archetypal elements of the **collective unconscious**. *See also* **Jung, Carl Gustav**; **Little Dream**.

Chester Beatty Papyrus: An ancient Egyptian papyrus, found in Thebes and dating back to 2000 BCE, believed to be the first known recorded work of dream interpretation. Experts say it was written by priests of the god Horus (god of the sun, the arts, music, and beauty; identified with the Greek deity Apollo). The work indexes and interprets roughly two hundred distinct dreams, often ascribing a meaning that represents the complete opposite of the dream content—a method Freud would later employ with his **reversals**. *See also **Freud, Sigmund***.

Circadian Rhythm: Essentially, the internal body clock that runs on a twenty-four-hour cycle, regulating the sleeping and eating patterns of humans (and of all animals). These rhythms are influenced by such factors as sunlight and temperature and are highly adaptive to changing circumstances.

Collective Unconscious: For Jung, the deepest layer of the human psyche, and the one that connects us to the rest of humanity and to ancestors throughout history. Jung believed that dreams were not merely expressions of personal experience; they reflexively drew upon the connection to a universal wellspring of knowledge and experience. This knowledge was expressed in the dream world through characters and situations called **archetypes**. *See also **Jung, Carl Gustav***.

Condensation: In dreams, the unconscious process by which several thoughts are collapsed into a single symbol or image. Freud believed that this was one of two primary methods by which people repressed their unconscious urges. *See also **Displacement; Freud, Sigmund***.

Day Residue: Freud's term for the "leftover" thoughts and impressions picked up during the day that find their way into our dreams at night, usually as a substitute expression of more troubling and deep-seated issues. *See also **Dream Work; Freud, Sigmund; Manifest Content***.

Delaney, Gayle: A psychologist and founding president of the International Association for the Study of Dreams. Delaney pioneered the **dream interview** method of interpretation.

Displacement: For Freud, the way in which disturbing thoughts or urges are transferred onto seemingly innocuous or random dream images. Often, such images cause a disproportionate amount of anxiety and stress. Freud believed that displacement was one of two primary methods by which people repressed their unconscious minds' wishes. *See also* **Condensation;** **Freud, Sigmund**.

Dream Interview: A method for interpreting dreams developed by psychologist and author Gayle Delaney. With this method, the dreamer must recount the setting, main characters, important objects, and plot of the dream, describing each element as if speaking to someone from another planet who has no familiarity with the items and events described. After explaining the dream, the goal is to relate each element back to the dreamer's own life until an epiphany is reached and the dreamer understands the nature of the dream's very personal meaning. *See also* **Delaney, Gayle**.

Dream Work: For Freud, the process through which the unconscious mind disguises and censors the true meaning of a dream, turning the **latent content** into **manifest content**. Freud believed this to be a necessary mental function, because the latent content of a dream was too traumatic for the dreamer's conscious mind to acknowledge and process. *See also* **Freud, Sigmund**.

Ego: For Freud, the part of the personality that is conscious, most directly controls behavior, and is linked to external reality. The ego is often portrayed as the "mediator" that tries to balance the needs of the unconscious and instinctual **id** with those of the repressive, guilt-plagued **superego**. *See also* **Freud, Sigmund**.

Electra Complex: The unconscious urge of a young girl to have sex with her father. Freud coined the term, named for the character of Electra, daughter of King Agamemnon in Greek mythology. After her mother, Clytemnestra, conspired with her lover to kill Agamemnon, Electra and her brother, Orestes, joined forces to murder both their mother and her lover. The equivalent urge in males is called the **Oedipus complex**. *See also **Freud, Sigmund***.

Empty Chair Technique: A treatment method developed by Fritz Perls to help integrate distinct parts of a patient's personality. Two chairs are placed facing each other. The patient sits in one chair and, after describing aspects or characters from a dream, is encouraged to act out a dialogue with these aspects or characters by speaking to the empty chair. Later, the patient switches chairs and tries to respond from the perspective of the characters first spoken to. Perls believed that the "occupants" of the empty chair were aspects of the patient's own personality, and in encouraging the dialogue, he could help the patient assimilate disparate or unwelcome parts of the personality. *See also **Gestalt Therapy; Perls, Fritz; Top Dog/Underdog***.

Free Association: An interview technique Freud used to help patients understand the **latent content** of a dream. Patients described their dreams, and then Freud asked them to articulate whatever came to mind when thinking about the dream and its symbols. *See also **Freud, Sigmund***.

Freud, Sigmund (1856–1939): Psychiatrist and founder of modern **psychoanalysis**. Freud's major revelation was that the mind harbored **unconscious** motivations for behavior, and that those motivations were, for the most part, a mystery (although in his writings, he argues strongly that the primary motivation for all human behavior is the **libido**, or sexual instinct). In attempting to solve that mystery, Freud employed several indirect methods, among them **free association** and dream interpretation. In his seminal work, *The Interpretation of Dreams*, he describes his theory that the unconscious uses the dream world to express buried or repressed emotions—although the unconscious mind simultaneously attempts to disguise these emotions by misremembering the content of the dream—and that all dreams were expressions of **wish fulfillment**. Freud's method for treating mental illness has been considered a failure, and modern-day psychiatry discounts the disproportionate importance Freud placed on sexual urges as the motivating factor behind all conscious behavior. But his work is still considered revolutionary in its transformation of the way we talk about the inner workings of the human mind.

Gestalt Therapy: A school of thought founded by Fritz Perls, who believed that all aspects of a dream represented parts of the dreamer's personality. With Gestalt, Perls strove for an integrative approach to dream interpretation, using role-playing and imaginary dialogues with dream characters to help patients identify internal conflicts and achieve resolution. The goal was to integrate the parts into the whole. The word *gestalt* is German for "figure." *See also* ***Empty Chair Technique; Perls, Fritz; Top Dog/Underdog.***

Hippocrates (c. 460–377 BCE): Greek physician—considered the father of medicine—and firm believer in the phenomenon of **prodromal dreams**. Hippocrates also believed that dreams were messages sent from the gods.

Id: For Freud, the part of the psyche that is home to unconscious, primitive, sexual impulses (primarily the **libido**), and the part that seeks immediate gratification. Freud believed that the id was wholly inaccessible to the conscious mind; only through **psychoanalysis** and a careful decoding of a patient's dream content could one gain insight into the workings of the id. *See also **Ego**; **Freud, Sigmund**; **Superego***.

Imhotep: In ancient Egypt, the god of healing. Imhotep, a mere mortal, was an architect who was also skilled at medicine. The gods rewarded his talent by granting him immortality. Imhotep was thought to visit people during sleep to heal them or advise on medical matters. The Greek version of Imhotep was **Aesculapius**. *See also **Bes**; **Incubation***.

Incubation: Any of several practices—including, but not limited to, fasting, meditation, and ingestion of tonics or hallucinogens—intended to induce healing or advisory dreams. Incubation was a common practice in ancient Egypt and Greece, where supplicants presented offerings at temples devoted to the gods of dreaming and healing and slept in the temple until a dream was visited upon them. *See also **Aesculapius**; **Bes**; **Imhotep***.

Individuation: The striving toward psychological maturity, a unified personality, and higher consciousness. For Jung, individuation was the primary life goal. *See also **Jung, Carl Gustav***.

Jung, Carl Gustav (1875–1961): Once a disciple of Freud, Jung broke off to develop his own theories of the unconscious and methods of treatment in analytic psychology. Jung rejected Freud's notion that sexual urges were the underlying cause of all human behavior. He considered the human psyche a wellspring of potential, and he sought to understand its inner workings through a rigorous study of myth, spirituality, and dreams. Unlike Freud, he believed that dreams existed not to conceal but to reveal how the unconscious operated. The goal, for Jung, was to achieve greater self-awareness and **individuation**. While navigating the path toward self-awareness, however, each person grappled not just with individual experience, but with the larger arc of history and civilization as well. Jung believed that at the psyche's deepest level there was a **collective unconscious**—an imprinted symbolic language of **archetypes** expressed in dreams and meant to foster a greater enlightenment. Interestingly, haunting dreams hounded Jung at various times in his life, and some modern scholars have posited that he might have suffered from schizophrenic episodes. *See also* **Freud, Sigmund**.

Latent Content: For Freud, the latent content was the "true" (and often traumatic) meaning of a dream—a meaning disguised by the censoring of the **dream work**. Freud believed that a patient's latent dream content was usually some repressed wish of an infantile or sexual nature. *See also* **Freud, Sigmund***; **Manifest Content**.

Libido: The sexual instinct, what Freud called one of the two primary life forces. The other is **Thanatos**, or the death instinct. For Freud, the libido was the stronger and more important of the two. *See also* **Freud, Sigmund**.

Little Dream: For Jung, a dream with a primarily personal meaning. *See also* **Big Dream***; **Jung, Carl Gustav**.

Lucid Dreaming: A learned technique in which the dreamer retains some measure of consciousness during sleep in order to control the content and progression of a dream as it unfolds. Some dream experts believe that lucid dreams can reap great emotional benefits by helping us to conquer emotional fears or anxiety.

Mandala: In Hindu and Buddhist philosophy, any depiction of the universe from a human perspective. Such representations are often used to focus the mind's attention during meditation. For Jung, a mandala was some form of circular symbol that expressed the unity of the **Self**. Mandalas appear in dreams and take on different forms for different people. As one progresses along the path of **individuation**, the mandala's form becomes more complex. *See also* ***Jung, Carl Gustav***.

Manifest Content: The content of a dream as it is remembered upon waking. Freud believed the manifest content was merely a smoke screen, and that the mind reflexively repressed and disguised the latent (or unconscious) meaning of the dream. *See also* ***Freud, Sigmund***; ***Latent Content***.

Miller, Gustavus Hindman (1857–1929): Author of the popular 1901 dream dictionary *What's in a Dream* (now more commonly referred to as *10,000 Dreams Interpreted*). Though Miller wrote contemporaneously with Freud, his dream philosophy predates the insights of both Freud and Jung. He took an allegorical approach to dream interpretation, deconstructing the meaning of individual dream symbols large and small, with results both quaint ("For a young woman to dream of wearing a sprig of myrtle foretells to her an early marriage with a well-to-do and intelligent man") and absurd ("Coconuts in dreams warn of fatalities in our expectations, as sly enemies are encroaching upon your rights in the guise of ardent friends").

Neurosis: For Freud, symptoms related to the failure to effectively repress one's unconscious thoughts and urges, either through **condensation** or **displacement**. *See also **Freud, Sigmund***.

Nightmares: Dreams of helplessness or danger that induce fear, anxiety, and stress. Unlike **night terrors**, nightmares are always vividly remembered upon waking.

Night Terrors: A phenomenon, common in children, in which you wake, screaming and terrified, from a dream you do not remember. Strangely, night terrors most often occur not during **REM sleep**, but in deeper sleep. Often, the dreamer reports extreme disorientation, and sometimes paralysis, upon waking; as with sleepwalking, it is often hard to wake up someone suffering from night terrors. Night terrors can occur in adults as well, often at times of extreme emotional stress. *See also **Nightmares***.

Oedipus Complex: The unconscious urge of a young boy to have sex with his mother. Freud coined the term, named for the character Oedipus in Greek mythology. Oedipus, king of Thebes, unknowingly fulfilled a prophecy made before his birth in which he killed his father and married his mother. The equivalent urge in females is called the **Electra complex**. *See also **Freud, Sigmund***.

Oneirocriticism: The practice of dream interpretation.

Perls, Fritz (1893–1970): Psychiatrist and founder of **Gestalt therapy**. *See also **Empty Chair Technique***.

Persona: One of Jung's four major **archetypes**; the face that a person displays to the outside world, not to be confused with the **Self**. *See also **Anima; Animus; Jung, Carl Gustav; Shadow**.*

Phallic Symbol: For Freud, anything in dream or waking life that symbolizes male genitalia—trains, big cigars, tree trunks, weapons, etc. *See also **Freud, Sigmund**.*

Preconscious: An early term Freud employed to describe parts of the psyche that are accessible to the conscious mind, but that might not currently be needed. This stands in opposition to the **unconscious**, a part of the psyche that is either repressed from or simply not accessible to the conscious mind. Over time, Freud's understanding of the human mind evolved from the three-part conscious/unconscious/preconscious construct to the **ego/id/superego** division of the psyche. *See also **Freud, Sigmund**.*

Prodromal Deams: Dreams thought to warn of the onset of disease or the presence of illness. Some dream analysts believe that while we sleep, the brain picks up on internal information that is cloaked or drowned out in waking life and transmits this information through a dream. For an example, see "Mechanical Malfunction," p. 158.

Projection: For Freud, the disavowal of one's dangerous or distasteful urges by ascribing them to another person, creating a comfortable psychic distance that allows a person to sit in judgment of the "other." *See also **Freud, Sigmund**.*

Psychoanalysis: The school of psychiatric treatment, founded by Sigmund Freud, which seeks to reveal the unconscious motivations for behavior through therapist-patient dialogues relating to dreams and childhood memories. *See also **free association**; **Freud, Sigmund***.

Regression: The psychological backslide to childish behavior and thoughts. Freud believed that when powerful desires were decisively thwarted by external forces, individuals often regressed to an earlier stage of development. Regression, if accompanied by **repression**, led to **neurosis**. If regression occurred without repression of one's sexual urges, Freud believed it led to what he called "perversion." *See also **Freud, Sigmund***.

REM (Rapid Eye Movement) Sleep: Also known as Stage 1 sleep, the stage during which dreaming most often occurs in humans. It is so named because researchers noticed that during this stage not only do the eyes dart back and forth under the lids, but respiration, pulse, and blood pressure fluctuate wildly as well. Paradoxically, despite the increased brain and eye activity during this stage, the body almost always remains completely still. REM sleep is actually the "lightest" and least restful of the four stages of sleep. As morning nears, the time spent in REM sleep grows longer—one reason why we are more likely to remember the dreams we have just before waking. *See also **Sleep Stages***.

Repression: The process by which a person "forgets" or unconsciously buries primal urges. Repression is a behavior most often associated with the **superego**. *See also **Freud, Sigmund***.

Reversal: A technique Freud used in analyzing dreams in which he would interpret a patient's activity, thought, or feeling in terms of its exact opposite. He believed that reversals helped to combat and cancel out the reflexive censorship that the unconscious mind performs when "remembering" a dream. *See also **Freud, Sigmund***.

Self: For Jung, one of the four main **archetypes**, and the one that represents the totality of the psyche and the full reservoir of human potential. *See also **Anima; Animus; Jung, Carl Gustav; Persona; Shadow***.

Serapea: In ancient Egypt and Greece, the name given to temples honoring gods that watched over dreams. *See also **Incubation***.

Shadow: For Jung, the **archetype** that represents the "dark" part of the personality, or the part kept hidden from the rest of the world. Although the Shadow is often difficult for a person to acknowledge, it can also symbolize untapped potential—a part of the personality that has heretofore not been allowed full expression. *See also **Anima; Animus; Jung, Carl Gustav; Persona; Self***.

Sleep Stages: Researchers have identified four distinct stages of the sleep process, distinguished by the types of brain waves measured with an electroencephalograph, or EEG machine. They range from Stage 1, also called **REM sleep** (the lightest or least restful stage and a time when the brain is most active and dreaming most common), to Stage 4, the deepest sleep, when the body enters an almost comalike state. Throughout a night of sleep, people periodically cycle, or "descend," through the four stages, from Stage 1/REM down to Stage 4 and back up again. As morning nears, the time spent in REM sleep grows longer—one reason why we are more likely to remember the dreams we have just before waking. *See also **Sleepwalking***.

Sleepwalking: A common variety of somnambulism, a disorder in which a person initiates activity while still asleep—anything from walking, talking, eating, or dressing to even driving a car. A sleepwalker's eyes are open during the activity, but have a dazed, unseeing look. The cause of sleepwalking is not known, but stress and excessive fatigue are thought to contribute to these incidents. Surprisingly, although increased brain and eye activity is a common feature of **REM sleep** (or Stage 1 sleep), sleepwalking most often occurs during deep (non-REM, nondreaming) sleep. A common old wives' tale states that it is dangerous or unhealthy to wake up a sleepwalker, but that statement has no basis in fact. The only danger posed by sleepwalking is a possible injury caused by falling or bumping into something. *See also Sleep Stages*.

Sublimation: For Freud, the attempt to harness the **libido** and redirect sexual urges into more "acceptable" social outlets. Freud hypothesized that this was the key to the rise of civilization, although he noted that sublimation is never completely attainable, because it's not possible to keep the libido under complete control. *See also Freud, Sigmund*.

Superego: For Freud, one of the three aspects of the personality, along with the **id** and the **ego**. Of the three, the superego is the "police officer," charged with imposing moral restrictions and reacting with severe repression against the primal sexual urges of the id. Freud believed dreams often depicted the superego in images of a father or other authority figure. *See also Freud, Sigmund*.

Thanatos: In ancient Greece, the god of death; his brother, Hypnos, was the god of sleep. Freud coined the term to describe the death instinct, the yearning to return to a state of stasis, or nonexistence—what he called one of two primary life forces. The other is the sexual instinct, or the **libido**, the stronger and more important of the two. *See also* ***Freud, Sigmund.***

Theta Rhythm: The type of brain waves that occur during Stage 1/REM and Stage 2 sleep. Some researchers now believe that the purpose of dreaming is to give the brain the chance to convert or "consolidate" short-term memory and sensory stimulation (processes associated with the hippocampus) into areas of the brain concerned with conscious thought and long-term memory bank (most often associated with the neocortex). These researchers believe that theta brain waves, which arise during deep relaxation, are the conduit, as it were, for this memory transmission. *See also* ***REM Sleep; Sleep Stages***.

Top Dog/Underdog: A technique used in **Gestalt therapy**, in which the patient recounts a dream in order to identify the "top dog" (the superior or dominant personality) and "underdog" (the oppressed personality) in the dream. A central tenet of Gestalt therapy is that the top dog and underdog actually represent aspects of the dreamer's own personality. *See also* ***Empty Chair Technique; Perls, Fritz***.

Transference: For Freud, the unconscious redirection of a patient's emotions, conflicts, or aggressions from one object or person to another. For example, in working through feelings of loss at the end of an affair, a patient might develop romantic feelings for the therapist. Freud believed that transference was a useful tool during analysis, as a means of gaining insight into a patient's childhood experiences. *See also* ***Freud, Sigmund; Projection***.

Unconscious: The part of the psyche not accessible to observation but which exerts control over all human behavior and emotion. Freud believed it was not possible to know the unconscious directly, but that through various indirect means, it was possible to obtain information about the workings of the unconscious mind. One of those indirect means was in interpreting a patient's dreams, which he called the "royal road to the unconscious." *See also **Freud, Sigmund**.*

Wish Fulfillment: The underlying motivating force behind every dream, what Freud called "the solution to all dreams." Freud believed that every dream represented the desire to fulfill a wish, even if that wish were repressed, hidden, or disguised. *See also **Freud, Sigmund**.*

Sources

Artemidorus. *Interpretation of Dreams: Oneirocritica*. Translated and with commentary by Robert J. White. Park Ridge, New Jersey: Noyes, 1975.

Brothers Grimm. *Grimms' Fairy Tales*. Translated by E. V. Lucas, Lucy Crane, and Marian Edwardes. New York: Grosset & Dunlap, 1945.

Bulfinch, Thomas. *Bulfinch's Mythology*, Modern Library edition. New York: Random House.

Chiriac, Jean. *Dream Interpretation from Primitives to Sigmund Freud and C. G. Jung*. Translated by Mihaela Cristea, 2004. http://essays.freudfile.org/dream_int.pdf (accessed August 2, 2005).

Daniels, Victor. "Notes on Carl Gustav Jung." http://www.sonoma.edu/users/d/daniels/junglect.html (accessed August 16, 2005).

Delaney, Gayle. *All About Dreams*. San Francisco: HarperSanFrancisco, 1998.

———. *In Your Dreams*. San Francisco: HarperSanFrancisco, 1997.

Dirks, Tim. "The Greatest Films." http://www.filmsite.org (accessed September 2, 2005).

Electric Dreams Dream Sharing Temple. "Common Dreams Index." http://www.dreamgate.com/dream/library/common_dreams01.htm (accessed August 15, 2005).

Encyclopedia Britannica. "Rain Dance." http://www.britannica.com/eb/article-9062487 (accessed February 20, 2006).

Ennis, Maeve, and Jennifer Parker. *Get a Grip on Dreams.* New York, Barnes & Noble, 2003.

Faraday, Ann. *Dream Power.* New York: Berkley, 1972.

Felluga, Dino. "Modules on Freud: On the Unconscious." *Introductory Guide to Critical Theory.* West Lafayette, Indiana: Purdue University, November 28, 2003. http://www.purdue.edu/guidetotheory/psychoanalysis/freud2.html (accessed October 10, 2005).

Fordham, Frieda. "An Introduction to Jung's Psychology: Dreams and Their Interpretation." *The Jung Page.* http://www.cgjungpage.org/index.php?option=com_content&task=view&id=679&Itemid=41 (accessed July 24, 2005).

Freud, Sigmund. *The Interpretation of Dreams.* Translated and edited by James Strachey. New York: Avon, 1998.

———. "Psychopathology of Everyday Life." Translated by A. A. Brill. *Classics in the History of Psychology.* http://psychclassics.yorku.ca/Freud/Psycho/chap8.htm (accessed August 10, 2005).

Gibson, Clare. *The Secret Life of Dreams: Decoding the Messages from Your Subconscious*. San Diego: Thunder Bay, 2003.

Holloway, Gillian. *The Complete Dream Book*. Naperville, Illinois: Sourcebooks, 2001.

Ivin-Amar, Silvana. *Dream Lover, Inc.* http://www.dreamloverinc.com/home.htm (accessed August 16, 2005).

Jung, Carl Gustav. *Dreams*. Translated by R. F. C. Hull. Princeton, New Jersey: Princeton University Press, 1974.

Kantrowitz, Barbara, and Karen Springen. "What Dreams Are Made Of." *Newsweek*, August 9, 2004. http://www.msnbc.msn.com/id/5569228/site/newsweek/ (accessed December 10, 2005).

Keskinen, Mikko. "Hearing Voices in Dreams: Freud's Tossing and Turning with Speech and Writing." *PsyArt: An Online Journal for the Psychological Study of the Arts*, 2002 issue. http://www.clas.ufl.edu/ipsa/journal/2002_keskinen01.shtml (accessed October 10, 2005).

Klages, Mary. "Psychoanalysis and Sigmund Freud." September 27, 2001. http://www.colorado.edu/English/ENGL2012Klages/freud.html (accessed August 15, 2005).

Miller, Gustavus Hindman. *10,000 Dreams Interpreted*. New York: Barnes & Noble, 1996.

Myths-Dreams-Symbols: The Psychology of Dreams.
http://mythsdreamssymbols.com/index.shtml (accessed August 1, 2005).

Palmquist, Stephen. "Dreams of Wholeness: A Course of Introductory
Lectures on Psychology and Personal Growth."
http://www.hkbu.edu.hk/~ppp/dow/ (accessed October 4, 2005).

Ravenari. "Amara's Dream Dictionary."
http://www.ravenari.com/vilturr/runes/am1.html (accessed August, 3
2005).

Romanian Association for Psychoanalysis Promotion (AROPA). "Sigmund
Freud—Life and Work." http://www.freudfile.org/ (accessed August 2,
2005).

Taylor, Jeremy. "Articles on Dreams and Dreaming." *Jeremy Taylor: Dream
Work.* http://www.jeremytaylor.com/pages/dreamwork.html#Anchor-
Article-47082 (accessed August 15, 2005).

Thomson, Sandra. *Cloud Nine: A Dreamer's Dictionary.* New York:
Harper, 1999.

Wilkerson, Richard, and Peggy Coats. "Dream & Dreaming Links."
Dreamgate.com. http://www.dreamgate.com/dream/resources/online_a.htm
(accessed August 2, 2005).

Index

Numbers in **bold** (for example, **96**) can be used to locate dream images in the color plate section. All other numbers are page numbers.

A

Abraham (biblical figure), 189
accidents
    with airplane, **2b**, 8–11
    with boat, 8–11
    with car, **1b**, 8–11, 41–43
    with train, **1a**, 8–11
Adler, Alfred, 5, 239
adultery, **50**, 142–145, 182
The Adventures of Huckleberry Finn, 198–199
Aeschylus, 214
Aesculapius, 41, 239
An Affair to Remember, 63
aggression, symbols of
    jungle, 148–151
    monsters, 15, 33, 161–162
    war, 99, 229–230
    weapons, 233–236
AIDS patients, fire dreams in, 121
airplane connections, missed, 61–64
airplane disaster, **2b**, 8–11
airplane travel, **2a**, 11–13
alchemy, 96–97, 123, 128–129
Alice's Adventure's in Wonderland, 53

aliens, **3**, 13–17
amplification, 239–240
amputation, 113, 116–117, 236–237
angels, **4**, 16–17
Anima, 183, 240
    representations of
        death, 75–76, 80
        female gods as, 35
        mud/earth, 170
        water, 30, 37, 63, 83, 86, 174–175, 195–196, 198, 219, 232
Anima intellectualis, 40
animal(s), 21–24
    attack by wild, **5**, 17–21
    being chased by, 48–49
    domestic, **6b**, 21
    exotic, **6a**, 21
    jungle, 148–151
    talking, 24
animal fur, 130
Animus, 182–183, 240
    representations of
        death, 75–76, 80

male gods as, 35
police officers, 185
ants, 147
anxiety dreams
airplane travel, 12
brain, 39
dental (teeth), 167–168,
220–221
exam/public performance,
101–103
falling, 107–109
lost purse or wallet, 193–194
missed connections, 61–64
vehicular accidents, 9
Aphrodite, 189
apocalypse, **34**, 98–101, 229
archetypes, Jungian, 5, 240, 242,
247, 250, 252
Aristotle, 3
Artemidorus, 3–4, 97, 126, 168,
221, 224, 240–241
association, free, 244
astral projection, 241
Athena, 189
attack by wild animal, **5**, 17–21
attic, **7**, 24–26
auditory hallucinations, 90
authority figures, police officers as,
183–186
automobiles. *See* cars

B
Babylonians, 133–134, 209
Baker, Joe Don, 235
baldness (hair loss), **44b**, 129–132
basement, **8**, 26–28
bathrooms, **33**, 94–98
bathtub as vehicle, **82a**, 227
beach, **9**, 28–31
bears, 20, 22
bed, something under, **10**, 31–34
bed-wetting, symbols of
fire, 122–123
water, 30, 83, 174, 195, 198,
219, 232
bees, 146–147
Bes (Egyptian god), 3, 40–41, 241
biblical figures, **11**, 34–36
Abraham and Sarah, 189
angels, 4, 16–17
Jacob, 93–94
Samson, 105, 131–132
big dream (Jungian), 241
bile, 155
Bill & Ted's Excellent Adventure,
135–136
birth, giving, **66**, 187–189
birth trauma, 237–238
blindness, 104–106
blood (wounds), 236–238
boats, **12**, 36–38, 63

accident with, 8–11
missed connections, 61–64
river travel, 197–199
as symbol for uterus, 9
body, burying, 66–67
body parts
brain, **13**, 39–41
ears, **31**, 87–90
eyes, **36**, 103–107
feet, **39a**, 112–116
fingers, **40**, 116–120
hands, **40**, 116–120
heart, **45**, 132–134
legs, **39a**, 112–116
liver, **54**, 153–155
bombs, 233–236
brain, **13**, 39–41
breathing underwater, **30**, 84–87
broken glass, **43**, 126–129
Bronson, Charles, 235
Brothers Grimm, 33–34, 53
Buddha, 34
Buffy the Vampire Slayer, 162
bullets, 234
buried treasure, **80**, 222–225
burned, being, **41**, 120–124
Burroughs, Edgar Rice, 151
burying dead body, 66–67
butterflies, **51b**, 146–148

C

Callisto, 207
caesarean section, 189
cancer patients, fire dreams in, 121
Candy, John, 63
cars
accident with, **1b**, 8–11
illogical use of, **82b**
missed connections, 61–64
as phallic symbol, 159
trouble with, **14**, 41–43,
158–160
cats, **6b**
cave, **15**, 43–46
celebrities, 46–48
in everyday life, **16b**
on red carpet, **16a**
Changing Woman (Navajo), 171
Charlie and the Chocolate Factory,
90–91
chased, being, **17**, 48–51
by wild animal, 17–24
Chester Beatty papyrus, 3, 168,
221, 241–242
child(ren)
desire for, losing teeth as symbol
for, 168, 221
discovering, **18a**
forgetting or misplacing, **18b**,
51–53

childhood home, **47**, 136–138

Christianity, 4

Churchill, Winston, **46b**, 134

circadian rhythm, 242

city, **19**, 53–55

Cleopatra, **46a**, 134

clothing, 177

clubs (weapons), 233–236

cognitive therapy, 5, 239

collective unconscious, 5, 241–242, 247

communication breakdown, **20**, 55–57, 156

compensation, theory of, 72

computers, **21**, 57–61

condensation, 242, 249

connections, missed, **22**, 61–64

corridors, **23a**, 64–66

crashes, **1a, 1b, 2b**, 8–11

creation myths, 171–172

crime

  committing, **24**, 66–70

  victim of, **25**, 70–73

crocodiles, 21

Cupid, 217

D

dark center (Jungian), 19, 24, 147

da Vinci, Leonardo, 12–13

day residue, 40, 242

dead body, burying, 66–67

deafness, 89–90

death

  of father, 110–111

  of loved one (unrelated to actual death), **26**, 73–76

  of mother, 163–165

  ravens as symbol of, 23

  your own, **27**, 76–78

Death Wish, 235

death wish/instinct, 247, 253

  vehicular accidents and, 9, 42, 227–228

deceased loved one, visit from, **28**, 79–81

defecation

  inappropriate or inconvenient, **33**, 94–98

  mud as symbol for, 170

  as symbol for money, 223

Delaney, Gayle, 242–243

Delilah, 131–132

De Niro, Robert, 47–48

dental anxiety, 167–168, 221–222

De Palma, Brian, 235–236

desert island, 81–84

  peaceful, **29a**, 82

  sinister, **29b**, 82–83

Deuteronomy, 144

diagnostic power of dreams, 154

Dietrich, Marlene, 210

Dirty Harry, 235

disasters
end of the world, **34**, 98–101, 229
natural, **61**, 172–175, 232

displacement, 243, 249

dogs, **6b**, 22–23

domestic animals, **6b**, 21

Donne, John, 83–84

dragon, 160–161

dream(s). *See also specific types*
big (Jungian), 241
biological purpose of, 2
diagnostic power of, 154
as guardians of sleep, 89, 230
little (Jungian), 247
lucid, 7, 247–248
prodromal, 245, 250
as royal road to unconscious, 4, 255

dream analysis
do-it-yourself, 6–7
history of, 3–5

dream catcher, 148

dream interview, 242–243

dream journal, 6–7

dream reversals, 141, 144, 182, 241–242, 251–252

dream temples, 3, 40–41, 252

dream work, 216, 243, 247

driving problems, **14**, 41–43, 158–160

drowning, **30**, 28, 84–87, 231

E

ears, **31**, 87–90

earth (mud), 169–172

earthquakes, **61**, 172–175, 232

Eastwood, Clint, 235

Ecstasy, 210

ego, 243

Egyptian mythology, eye imagery in, 105–106

Egyptians, ancient, 3
burial gift (*ka*), 93
Chester Beatty papyrus, 3, 168, 221, 241–242
dream temples, 3, 40–41, 252
fertility/sex rites, 209
god of dreams (Bes), 3, 40–41, 241
god of healing (Imhotep), 40–41, 246
incubation by, 3, 246
Stairway of Seven Planets, 93

Electra (Sophocles), 214

Electra complex, 111, 164–165, 213, 244

Electra myth, 214

elephants, 23

elevators, **32**, 90–94

elimination, inappropriate or inconvenient, **33**, 94–98

empty chair technique, 244

endless staircases, **23b**, 64

end of the world, 34, 98–101, 229

Epic of Gilgamesh, 151

erroneously carried-out actions, 128

Escher, M. C., 91

Esperanto, 57

evil eye, 106–107, 119–120

exam, **35b**, 101–103

excrement
    inappropriate or inconvenient, **33**, 94–98
    mud as symbol for, 170
    as symbol for money, 223

exotic animals, **6a**, 21

eyes, **36**, 103–107

F

fairy tales, 33–34, 53

falling, **37**, 78, 107–109
    and actual death, fallacy about, 78, 107

famous people
    biblical figures, **11**, 16–17, 34–36
    celebrities, **16a**, **16b**, 46–48
    historical figures, **46a**, **46b**, 134–136

father, **38**, 109–112
    death of, 110–111
    sex with, 111, 213–214, 244
    Spiritual Father (Jungian), 112, 183

feces
    inappropriate or inconvenient elimination, **33**, 94–98
    mud as symbol for, 170
    as symbol for money, 223

feet, **39a**, 112–116

feminine archetypes, 183, 240
    death, 75–76, 80
    female gods as, 35
    mud/earth, 170
    water, 30, 37, 63, 83, 86, 174–175, 195–196, 198

fertility rites, 209

fight-or-flight response, 109

fingers, **40**, 116–120

fire, **41**, 120–124

firewalking, 123–124

Fitzherbert, Maria, 201–202

floating, 85

flood, 231

flying, **42**, 124–126
    via airplane, **2a**, 11–13

foot binding, 115–116

footprints, **39b**, 113–114

Ford, Harrison, 50

Foster, Jodie, 47–48

Fragment of an Analysis of a Case of Hysteria, 122–123

free association, 244

freedom, symbols of
  airplane, 11
  feet, 115–116
  flying, 124–126
  teeth falling out, 168, 221

Freud, Sigmund, 4–5, 244–245
  on angels, 17
  on attic, 25
  on basement, 27
  on birth, 188
  on birth trauma, 237–238
  on body parts, 133
  on brain, 40
  on buried treasure (money), 223
  on caves, 45
  on chased, being, 50, 115
  on city, 54
  on communication, 56
  on crime commission, 68
  on crime victim, 71–72
  on death of loved one, 75
  on death of self, 77–78
  on diagnostic power, 154
  on drowning, 86
  on ears, 89
  on erroneously carried-out actions, 128
  on exam/public performance, 103
  on eyes/blindness, 105
  on falling, 108
  on father, 111
  on fingers and hands, 118–119
  on fire, 122–123
  on flying, 125
  on frustration, 59
  on hair/fur, 130
  on historical figures, 47, 135
  on impossible task, 141
  on infantile material for dreams, 137
  on infidelity, 144
  on insects/vermin, 147
  on jungle, 150
  on kitchens, 152
  on lost, being, 156
  on lost purse or wallet, 193–194
  on mechanical malfunction, 159
  on missed connections, 63
  on monsters, 14–15, 33, 161–162
  on mother, 164–165
  on mouth and teeth, 167–168, 220–221
  on mud, 170
  on natural disasters, 174

on open doorways, 65

on paralysis/inability to run, 115, 179

on police officers, 185

on public nudity, 177

on punishment, 59, 141, 191

on religious icons, 35

on rooms, 25, 27, 152, 200–201, 203

on sex/gender reversal, 205

on sex in public, 209

on sex interruption, 207

on sex with someone you know (not your partner), 213

on sex with stranger, 216

on staircases, 65, 92–93

on swamp, 219

on tunnel, 226

on urination and defecation, 96, 223

on vehicles/transportation, 9, 12, 37, 42, 227–228

on visit from deceased loved one, 80

on volcanoes, 174

on war, 99, 229–230

on water, 30, 83, 86, 174, 195, 198, 219, 232

on weapons, 235

on wild animals, 19, 23, 150

on wounds, 237–238

frustration dreams
    computer, 57–61
    impossible task, 140–142
    interrupted sex, 206–207

The Fugitive, 50–51

G

gay sex, 204–205

gender reversal, **73**, 204–205

Genesis, 93–94, 171

George IV, 201–202

Gestalt therapy, 245, 254

ghost
    sex with, **77**, 215–216
    visit from deceased loved one, **28**, 79–81

glass, broken, **43**, 126–129

Grant, Cary, 63

Great Mother (Jungian), 35, 165, 183

Greek mythology
    birth imagery, 157
    Cupid and Psyche, 217
    Electra, 214, 244
    Minotaur, 65–66
    Odysseus (Ulysses), 157
    Oedipus, 213–214, 249
    Prometheus, 155
    Thanatos, 253–254

Zeus and his lovers, 207
Greeks, ancient, 3
    Artemidorus, 3–4, 97, 126, 168,
       221, 224, 240–241
    cities, 55
    dream temples, 3, 40–41, 252
    elimination habits, 97
    fertility/sex rites, 209
    incubation by, 3, 41, 246
grenades, 234
guardians of sleep, dreams as, 89,
    230
guns, **85**, 233–236

H

hair, 129–132
    abundant, **44a**, 130
    loss of, **44b**, 129–132
hallucinogens, 246
hallways, **23a**, 64–66
Hamlet, 80–81
hamsa, 106–107, 119–120
handcuffs, 116–118
hands, **40**, 116–120
hatchet, 235
Hawthorne, Nathaniel, 145
Hays Code, 210
hearing (ears), **31**, 87–90
heart, **45**, 132–134
Hera, 207

Heyerdahl, Thor, 38
Hinckley, John, Jr., 47–48
Hippocrates, 245
historical figures, **46a**, **46b**,
    134–136
Hitchcock, Alfred, 27–28, 186
home, childhood, **47**, 136–138
Homer, 157
homosexual-heterosexual reversal,
    204–205
homosexual sex in public, 209–210
Horus, 106
hospital, **48**, 138–140
house
    attic, 24–26
    basement, 26–28
    childhood, **47**, 136–138
    corridors/hallways, **23a**, 64–66
    kitchen, **53**, 151–153
    as mansion of soul, 25, 65, 137
    as metaphor for Self, 25–27, 65,
       137, 152–153, 201, 203
    secret rooms, **71**, 199–202
    unused rooms, **72**, 202–204
Hughes, John, 63
Humphreys, Laud, 209–210
hurricanes, 172–175
husband (spouse), **64**, 181–183
    infidelity to, **50**, 142–145, 182

sex with someone other than, **76**, 143, 211–214

I

icons, religious, **11b**, 16, 34–36
id, 243, 246
ideas, airplane as symbol of, 11–12
Iktomi, 148
I Love Lucy, 159–160
Imhotep, 40–41, 246
impossible task, **49**, 140–142
impotence, fear of, 59, 141, 159
incest, 111, 163–165, 213–214, 244, 249
incubation, 3, 41, 246
independence, feet as symbols of, 115–116
Independence Day, 15
individuation, 246–247
inferiority complex, 239
infestation, insect, **51a**, 145–158
infidelity, **50**, 142–145, 182
In Search of Lost Time, 138
insects, 145–148
  appealing, **51b**
  infestation, **51a**
intellectual spirit, 40
internal dream censor, 77–78
The Interpretation of Dreams, 4, 245
interrupted sex, **74**, 182, 206–207

interview, dream, 242–243
Io, 207
Isaac (biblical figure), 189
Ishtar, 209
Islamic society, infidelity in, 145
isolation, on desert island, 81–84

J

Jacob's Ladder, 93–94
jail (prison), **67**, 190–192
Janssen, David, 50–51
Jesus Christ, 34–35
Joan of Arc, 35–36, 123
John the Apostle, 100
Jones, Tommy Lee, 50
journal, 6–7
Julius Caesar, 189
Jung, Carl, 5, 246–247
  on alchemy, 96–97, 123, 128–129
  on angels, 17
  on attic, 25–26
  on basement, 27
  on birth, 188
  on blood/wounds, 238
  on boats, 37–38, 63
  on brain, 40
  on buried treasure, 224
  on caves, 45–46
  on celebrities, 47

on chased, being, 50
on city, 54–55
on corridors/hallways, 65
on crime commission, 68
on crime victim, 72
on death of loved one, 75–76
on death of self, 78
on desert island, 83
on drowning, 86
on earth/earthly nature, 170–171
on earthquakes, 174
on elevators, stairs, and ladders, 93
on end of the world, 99–100
on exam/public performance, 103
on eyes/blindness, 105
on falling, 108
on father, 112
on fingers and hands, 119
on fire, 123
on flying, 125
on frustration, 59–60
on glass container, 128–129
on hair, 131
on hearing, 90
on historical figures, 135
on hospital, 139–140
on house, 25–26, 65, 137, 152–153, 201, 203
on impossible task, 142

on infidelity, 144
on inner demons (aliens), 15
on insects, 147–148
on kitchen, 152–153
on liver, 154–155
on lost, being, 157
on lost or missing child, 53
on lost purse or wallet, 194
on mechanical malfunction, 159
on missed connections, 63
on mother, 165
on mouth and teeth, 168, 221
on natural disasters, 174–175
on paralysis, 180
on partner/spouse, 182–183
on police officers, 185
on primeval forest, 150
on prison, 191
on public nudity, 177
on religious icons, 35
on return to childhood, 137
on rivers, 198
on secret rooms, 201
on sex/gender reversal, 205
on sex in public, 209
on sex interruption, 207
on sex with someone you know (not your partner), 213
on sex with stranger, 216
on something under bed, 33

on swamp, 219
on transportation, 10, 12, 37–38, 43, 228
on tunnel, 226
on unused rooms, 203
on urination and defecation, 96–97
on visit from deceased loved one, 80
on walking, 115
on war, 230
on water, 30, 37, 83, 86, 174–175, 195–196, 198, 219
on weapons, 235
on wild animals, 19, 23–24, 150
jungle, **52**, 148–151
The Jungle Book, 151

K

ka, 93
Kafka, Franz, 186
Keaton, Buster, 159
Kerr, Deborah, 63
Kipling, Rudyard, 151
kitchen, **53**, 151–153
knives, **85**, 233–236
Kohlberg, Lawrence, 69–70
Kubrick, Stanley, 60

L

labyrinth, 65-66
ladders, 26, 65, 90–94
Lady Godiva, 177–178
lakes, 230. *See also* water
Lamarr, Hedy, 210
language, unfamiliar, 55–57, 156
late, fear of being, 61–64
latent content, 243–244, 247
Leda, 207
legs, **39a**, 112–116
    dysfunction of (paralysis), **63**, 48, 113–116, 178–180
leopards, 20
Leviticus, 144
The Libation Bearers, 214
libido, 244–245, 247
    symbols of
        chase, 50
        wild animals, 19, 23
Lindbergh, Charles, Jr., 53
little dream (Jungian), 247
liver, **54**, 153–155
loneliness, and desert island, 81–84
lost, being, **55**, 155–157
lost child, **18b**, 51–53
lost purse or wallet, **68**, 193–194
loved one
    death of (unrelated to actual death), **26**, 73–76

deceased, visit from, **28**, 79–81
lucid dreaming, 7, 247–248

M

Magnuson, Ann, 217
make love. *See also* sex
  nowhere to, 206–207
Making Mr. Right, 217
Malkovich, John, 217
mandala, 248
manifest content, 243, 248
mansion of soul, house as, 25, 65, 137
marital trouble, 142–145, 181–183
Martin, Steve, 63
Mary (mother of Jesus), **11**, 34–35
masculine archetypes, 182–183, 240
  death, 75–76, 80
  male gods, 35
  police officers, 185
masturbation, 167, 220
Mayans, 171–172, 196
maze, 64–66
mechanical malfunction, **56**, 158–160
memories, attic as symbol of, 24–25
Memories, Dreams, Reflections, 97, 99–100, 154–155
menopause, fire dreams in, 121
menstrual blood, 238

Mercury (planet), and communication, 57
messengers, angels as, 16–17
metropolis, 55
military artillery, 233–235
Miller, Gustavus Hindman, 176, 224, 248
Mimir, 106
Minotaur, 65–66
missed connections, **22**, 61–64
missing child, **18b**, 51–53
Mitchum, Robert, 73
money
  buried treasure, 222–225
  excrement as symbol of, 223
monsters, **57**, 160–163
  aliens as, 14–15
  under bed, 31–34
  being chased by, 48–49
  wild animals as, 22
moose, 20
moral development, stages of, 69–70
Moses, 34
mother, **58**, 163–165
  death of, 163–165
  environmental archetype of, 219
  Great Mother (Jungian), 35, 165, 183
  sex with, 163–165, 213–214,

249
   spiders as symbols of, 147
mountain lions, 20
mouth, **59**, 166–168
mud, **60**, 169–172
Mud People, 171
Muhammad, 34
myoclonic jerk, 108–109

N

nakedness, public, **62**, 175–178
Napoleon I, 229–230
Native Americans, 3
   creation myths, 171
   dream catchers, 148
   rain dances, 196
   spider deities, 148
   third eye, 106, 119
native civilizations, 3
natural disasters, **61**, 172–175, 232
Navajo culture, 148, 171
neurosis, 249
nightmares, 249
The Night of the Hunter, 72–73
night terrors, 249
Norse mythology, eye imagery in, 106
Nostradamus, 100
nowhere to make love, 206–207
nuclear holocaust, **34**, 98

nudity, public, **62**, 175–178
Nu Gua, 171

O

ocean, **9**, 28–31, 230
   drowning in, 84–87
   natural disasters, 173–174, 232
Odin, 106
The Odyssey, 157
Oedipus complex, 17, 27–28, 105, 111, 164–165, 213, 249
Oedipus myth, 213–214
Oedipus Rex, 213–214
Oneirocritica, 3, 224, 240–241
oneirocriticism, 249
Othello, 145
"outside the box" thinking, 142

P

palmistry, 119
paparuda, 196
Parable of Cave (Plato), 45–46
paralysis, **63**, 48, 113–116, 178–180
partner, **64**, 181–183
   infidelity to, **50**, 142–145, 182
   sex with someone other than, **76**, 143, 211–214
penguins, **6a**

Perls, Fritz, 5, 244–245, 249
Persona, 240, 250
  metaphors for
    celebrities, 47
    clothing, 177
    historical figures, 135
    lost purse or wallet, 194
phallic symbols, 250
  cars, 159
  city (skyscraper), 54
  fingers and hands, 118
  teeth, 167–168
  vehicles or transportation, 159,
    227–228
  weapons, 234–236
Phoenicians, 38
phoenix, 121–122
The Picture of Dorian Gray, 205
Planes, Trains & Automobiles, 63
Plato, 3, 45–46
police officers, **65**, 183–186
preconscious, 250
pregnancy, **66**, 187–189
  fear of, infanticide and, 68, 191
  insects/vermin as symbol of, 147
prison, **67**, 190–192
problem-solving dreams, 39–41
prodromal dreams, 245, 250
projection, 250
Prometheus, 155

prophets, 34–36
Proust, Marcel, 138
Psyche (Cupid's wife), 217
Psycho, 27–28, 186
psychoanalysis, 4–5, 244–246,
  250–251
Psychopathology of Everyday Life, 128
public nudity, **62**, 175–178
public performance, **35a**, 101–103
public sexual act, **75**, 181, 208–211
punishment dreams, 59, 141,
  190–192
purse, lost, **68**, 193–194

Q
quicksand, 169, 218

R
rafts, river travel via, 197–199
rain, **69**, 194–196
rain dances, 196
rapid eye movement (REM) sleep,
  2, 251
ravens, 23
Reagan, Ronald, 47–48
rebirth, 188
red carpet, celebrities on, **16a**
Reeves, Keanu, 135
regression, 251

religious icons, **11b**, 16, 34–36
Remembrance of Things Past, 138
REM sleep, 2, 251
Remus, 151
repressed urges, symbols of
   monsters, 14–15, 33, 161–162
   wild animals, 19, 22–23
repression, 251
The Republic, 45
Revelation, 100
reversals, Freudian, 141, 144, 182,
   241–242, 251–252
right side versus left side, 118–119
rivers, **70**, 197–199
roaches, 147
Romanian rite of *paparuda*, 196
Roman mythology, 151
Romans, ancient, 97–98, 153
Romanticism, 4
Romulus, 151
rooms
   attic, 24–26
   basement, 26–28
   kitchen, **53**, 151–153
   secret, 71, 199–202
   as symbol for women, 25, 27,
     152, 200–201, 203
   unused, **72**, 202–204
Royal Pavilion, 201–202
royal road to unconscious, 4, 255

running in slow motion, **63**, 48,
   178–180

S

Saint Joan, 123
saints, 34–36
same-sex encounter, 204–205
Samson, 105, 131–132
sand, 29–30
Sarah (biblical figure), 189
saviors, 34–36
The Scarlet Empress, 210
The Scarlet Letter, 145
scars, 236–238
Scherner, Karl, 133
scuba diving, 87
secret rooms, **71**, 199–202
seeing (eyes), **36**, 103–107
Self (Jungian), 240, 252
   metaphors for
     buried treasure, 224
     city, 54–55
     house, 25–27, 65, 137,
       152–153, 201, 203
     talking animals, 24
serapea (dream temples), 40–41,
   252
sex
   with father, 111, 213–214, 244
   with ghost, **77**, 215–216

homosexual-heterosexual reversal, 204–205
interrupted, **74**, 182, 206–207
with mother, 163–165, 213–214, 249
with partner/spouse, 181
in public, **75**, 181, 208–211
with someone you know (not your partner), **76**, 143, 211–214
with stranger, **77**, 143, 215–217
symbols of
  chase, 50
  crime victim, 72
  falling, 108
  lost purse or wallet, 193–194
  menstrual blood, 238
  monsters, 161–162
  paralysis/inability to run, 115, 179
  secret rooms, 201
  staircases, 65, 92–93
  teeth, 167–168, 220–221
  tunnel, 226
  unused rooms, 203
  urination, 96
  volcanoes, 174
  weapons, 234–236
  wild animals, 19, 23
sex/gender reversal, **73**, 204–205

Shadow self, representations of
celebrities, 47
chase, 50
committing crime, 68
historical figures, 135
homosexuality, 205
imprisonment, 191
insects, 147–148
police officers, 185
pursuer or hunter, 50
wild animals, 19, 23–24
Shakespeare, William, 80–81, 145
sharks, 21
Shaw, George Bernard, 123
shipwreck, 8, 36
shoes, **39a**, 112–116
sidedness, right versus left, 118–119
Siegel, Alan, 121, 204
sinking boat, 8, 36
skull, Jung on, 40
skyscraper, 54
sleep, rapid eye movement, 2, 251
sleep stages, 252
sleepwalking, 253
slow motion, running in, **63**, 178–180
snakes, 23
Sophocles, 213–214
speech
  airplane as symbol of, 11–12

Freud on, 89
unfamiliar or misunderstood, **20**, 55–57, 156
spider(s), 146–147
spider gods, 148
Spider Grandmother (Navajo), 148
Spiritual Father (Jungian), 112, 183
spouse, **64**, 181–183
    infidelity to, **50**, 142–145, 182
    sex with someone other than, **76**, 143, 211–214
staircases, endless, **23b**, 64
stairs, 26, 65, 90–94
Stairway of the Seven Planets, 93
Stekel, Wilhelm, 118–119
Stevenson, Robert Louis, 205
storms, 172–175
The Strange Case of Dr. Jekyll and Mr. Hyde, 205
stranger, sex with, **77**, 143, 215–217
sublimation, 253
suicide, 76
superego, 243, 253
    symbols of
        attic, 25
        crime victim, 71–72
        ears, 89
        police officers, 185
survival, jungle as symbol for, 148–151
swamp, **78**, 169, 218–219
swimming, 85, 176, 231

T

Talmud, 168, 221
Tarzan, 151
tears, rain as symbol for, 194
technology
    computers, **21**, 57–61
    mechanical malfunction, **56**, 158–160
teeth, **59**, 166–168
    falling out, **79**, 166–168, 219–222
temples, dream, 3, 40–41, 252
10,000 Dreams Interpreted, 248
terrors, night, 249
test (exam), **35b**, 101–103
Thanatos (death instinct), 247, 253
    vehicular accidents and, 9, 42, 227–228
theta rhythm, 254
third eye, 106, 119–120
tigers, 20
toilets, **33**, 94–98
top dog/underdog, 254
tornadoes, **61**, 172–175
trains
    accident with, **1a**, 8–11

missed connections, 61–64

passage through tunnel, 226

transference, 254

transportation

airplane disaster, **2b**, 8–11

airplane travel, **2a**, 11–13

boat accident, 8–11

boat travel, **12**, 36–38

car accident, **1b**, 8–11, 41–43

car trouble, **14**, 41–43, 158–160

Freud on, 9, 12, 37, 42, 227–228

illogical mode of, **82a**, 226–228

illogical use of vehicle, **82b**

Jung on, 10, 12, 37–38, 43, 228

missed connections, **22**, 61–64

phallic symbols in, 159, 227–228

train accident, **1a**, 8–11

tunnel, 225–226

via river, 197–199

trauma, birth, 237–238

travel. *See* transportation

treasure, buried, 80, 222–225

The Trial, 186

tsunami, 29, 173–174, 232

tunnel, **81**, 225–226

Twain, Mark, 198–199

2001: A Space Odyssey, 60

U

unconscious, 254–255

collective, 5, 241–242, 247

dialogue with, 6

Freud's royal road to, 4, 255

underwater breathing, **30**, 84–87

unused rooms, **72**, 202–204

urination, inappropriate or

inconvenient, **33**, 94–98

uterus, symbols for

cave, 44

purse, 193–194

vessels, 9, 37

water, 83, 195, 198, 219, 232

V

vagina, symbols for

cave, 45

open doorways, 65

purse or wallet, 193–194

tunnel, 226

vampire, 160–162

vehicles

airplane disaster, **2b**, 8–11

airplane travel, **2a**

boat accident, 8–11

boat travel, **12**, 36–38

car accident, **1b**, 8–11, 41–43

car trouble, **14**, 41–43

illogical mode of transportation,

82a, 226–228

illogical use of, **82b**

as phallic symbols, 159, 227–228

as symbol for uterus, 9, 37

train accident, **1a**, 8–11

victim of crime, **25**, 70–73

Virgin Mary, **11**, 34–35

vision (eyes), **36**, 103–107

visit, from deceased loved one, **28**

volcanoes, **61**, 172–175

W

walking, 112–116

Walking Tall, 235

wallet, lost, **68**, 193–194

War of the Worlds, 13

war zone, **83**, 99, 228–230, 236

water, **84**, 63, 83, 230–233

   beach/ocean, **9**, 28–31

   desert island, 81–84

   drowning, **30**, 28, 84–87, 231

   Freud on, 30, 83, 86, 174, 195, 198, 219, 232

   Jung on, 30, 37, 83, 86, 174–175, 195–196, 198, 219

   natural disasters, 172–175, 232

   rain, **69**, 194–196

   rivers, **70**, 197–199

   swamp, **78**, 169, 218–219

   travel via (boats), **12**, 36–38, 63

waves, 28–30, 173–174, 232

weapons, **85**, 233–236

werewolf, 160–161

What's in a Dream, 248

White Tara, 106

whitewater rapids, 197

wife (spouse), **64**, 181–183

   infidelity to, **50**, 142–145, 182

   sex with someone other than, **76**, 143, 211–214

wild animal, attack by, **5**, 17–21

Wilde, Oscar, 205

Winter, Alex, 135

Wise Old Man (Jungian), 24, 112, 183, 240

Wise Old Woman (Jungian), 240

wish fulfillment, 40, 245, 255

   childhood home, 137

   committing crime, 68

   death of loved one, 75

   sex in public, 209

   visit from deceased loved one, 80

wolves, 20, 151

womb. *See* uterus

women, symbols for, 183, 240

   death, 75–76, 80

   female gods as, 35

   heart, 134

   mud/earth, 170

   rooms, 25, 27, 152, 200–201, 203

   water, 30, 37, 63, 83, 86, 174–175,

195–196, 198, 219, 232
The Wonderful Wizard of Oz, 53
wounds, **86**, 236–238
Wright, Orville, 13
Wright, Wilbur, 13

Z

Zamenhof, L. L., 57
Zeus, 207

Acknowledgments

This book of dreams is dedicated to kb, who figures prominently in mine.

Thanks first and foremost to Mindy Brown for allowing a foot in the door, and to Erin Slonaker for working with patience and tireless good humor to make this book happen. Special thanks to Kevin Kosbab for his careful reading, Karen Onorato for her clean design and ingenious icons, and Derek Bacon for interpreting our dreams as works of art. Infinite gratitude to my friends and family, who offered encouragement and shared their dreams—particularly Leslie, with her wise, surprising insights into the dreaming mind. And a special hat-tipping to Bob O'Sullivan and Margot Weiss, whose steadfast support and sick senses of humor were completely not dispensable in the writing of this book.

More Quirk Field Guides

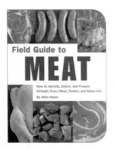
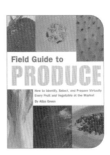
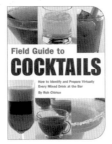
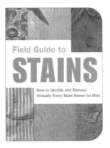